Acclaim for J. Arthur Holcombe's <u>*Path of Truth & Courage*</u>

The wisdom of Sir John Holcombe reaches into the hearts of many that elevate the words found in the pages of The Path of Truth & Courage, as life tools to teach their children and help with work and family issues.

"The Path of Truth & Courage moves the reader to want the goal of knighthood as much as Sir John himself, but in a carefully written plan, the goal changes and becomes the greatest lesson of love, loyalty and courage."

—K. Charles Cruz, Radio Ventana

"J. Arthur's literary talent transported me alongside Sir John as he was striving to become a man. After I read "The Path of Truth & Courage," I reread it afraid that I might have missed or forgotten a piece of wisdom. I have purchased at least a dozen other copies and have given them as presents to associates and friends."

—Caryne Edwards (Mother, wife, critical care nurse)

"This book should be required reading for young boys and girls who are in their formative years. Lessons are taught through every chapter of this book that can help mold a young person's character...."

—Randy Benge

"Whether you are the Lord of Dorchester, a Knight, corporate CEO, or stay at home mom; you will find yourself or someone you know in this book. The Path of Truth and Courage and the lessons taught in it … can be useful to anyone … this is a must read!"

—Irene Ruiz, Igosa.com

"Any epic is difficult to write, but an author who can pare down a story to less than 115 pages is a master of letters, in my opinion … the story is so well written it literally jumps off the page. It provides one with excellent entertainment, but also provides one with a type of encouragement and moral code that is rarely seen in modern self help books … Good show, Sir John!"

—John Tatum

The Path of Truth and Courage

The Path of Truth and Courage

✦

The Wisdom of Sir John Holcombe Knight, Crusader and Benevolent Lord of Dorchester

As Retold by J Arthur Holcombe

Writer's Showcase
New York Lincoln Shanghai

The Path of Truth and Courage
The Wisdom of Sir John Holcombe
Knight, Crusader and Benevolent Lord of Dorchester

Writer's Showcase
an imprint of iUniverse, Inc.

iUniverse books may be ordered through booksellers or by contacting:

iUniverse
2021 Pine Lake Road, Suite 100
Lincoln, NE 68512
www.iuniverse.com
1-800-Authors (1-800-288-4677)

Because of the dynamic nature of the Internet, any Web addresses or links contained in this book may have changed since publication and may no longer be valid.

The views expressed in this work are solely those of the author and do not necessarily reflect the views of the publisher, and the publisher hereby disclaims any responsibility for them.

Second Edition

ISBN: 978-0-595-21088-6

Printed in the United States of America

This book is dedicated to my loving wife and lifelong companion Geneva, who has shared all of my many failures and occasional successes but has remained faithful and patient; and my beautiful, exceptional children: my daughter Melissa and my son James.

All things are possible through Christ which strengthens me.
(Phil 4:13)

Contents

Foreword

♦

*Personal Testimonial
of
J. Arthur Holcombe*

In 1985, I left a faltering career with the Air Force to make my fortune in commercial real estate—just in time to experience the worst real estate market crash since the Great Depression. About a year later, I began experiencing stomach cramps that was diagnosed as ulcers. It made sense to me that I would have ulcers, with all I was going through. The developer I worked for was bleeding red ink when I joined them as Vice-President of Investments. I didn't know that until after we had nearly finished the new house and had moved out of the old one. They forced me out of the company a month before we were to close on our dream home. To make matters worse, the company's Savings and Loan was financing both the construction loan and the permanent financing. The cramps got progressively worse as we faced the stress of finishing the house and coming up with a way to pay for it. As each problem arose, a solution presented itself. We found the financing we needed to finish the house and move in, and fortunately (thanks to my wife, Geneva's intuition and persistence), I went into the Air Force Reserves straight out of active duty. Extra military duty gave us enough income to keep us afloat until I could find something more permanent.

Even though the problems were being solved, the cramps kept getting worse. The ulcer medication helped for awhile to ease the pain, but in time, the cramps came back much worse than before. In 1989, just as we were getting back on our feet, my health went into a nose dive. The night before I was hospitalized for advanced colon cancer, I came within hours of dying from a total blockage. After the emergency surgery, the doctors didn't have much hope of my leaving the hospital alive. They told Geneva that I would be lucky to live two weeks more.

It was years later that Geneva shared that prognosis with me. The recovery wasn't easy, but I never considered death as an option—I had too much to live for! My daughter was just 13 at the time, my son 12, plus my finances were in a total mess. For a year, I lived with a colostomy, endured 48 chemotherapy treatments, and went through a second abdominal surgery to reverse the colostomy. Through all of that, it occurred to me that I might not live to see my children become adults. I had so much I wanted to share with them, but there was the grim reality that I might not be there to do so. My decision to write "The Path of Truth and Courage" was to leave with my children some of the wisdom that had been passed down to me—to help them succeed in life if I couldn't be there to guide them.

I'm writing these reflections in the year 2007, so as Mark Twain once said, "the news of my death was greatly exaggerated." "The Path of Truth and Courage" was written entirely from the heart, and even though the principles in the book were intended to guide my children through life, those same words have helped me to live! And what a life it has turned out to be. In the first printing, I wrote on the cover that I was "a self-made millionaire and cancer survivor", but at the time, I was neither! Once the book had gone to the publisher, it was too late to change what was written, so I was committed to live by those words and prove that they were legitimate—if to no one else but my own family.

Today, by living the words written so long ago in "The Path of Truth and Courage", I can truthfully say I am both a cancer survivor and a multi-millionaire. I cannot say, however, that I am self-made. I must give credit where credit is due—I must give all the credit, thanks, and praise to God for making it all possible. He had a plan for me even though many of the experiences He led me through were painful. I've been blessed beyond my grandest dreams and now it's time to share those blessings with you. I encourage you to read and live by the wisdom tucked between the lines of the story. I also welcome you to write me and let me know if you've been helped by the message. I look forward to hearing from you.

J. Arthur Holcombe

(You can contact J. Arthur through his website at:
www.truthandcourage.com)

Reflections
of
Sir John Holcombe

The Story Begins

Reflections

To my beloved Wife, Sons, and Daughters,

Death, I fear, is close at hand. It is through a lifetime of mortal combat we struggle, only to ultimately lose our final battle to the Dark Knight. With the end drawing near, I pray to Almighty God that He grant me sufficient time and strength to complete this record. Compared to my vast worldly riches, I have nothing of greater value to leave than these final written treasures.

I leave my earthly possessions according to written instructions contained in my Final Will, but this I also give to you now, the most valuable of all the wealth I possess ... the final hours of my life. Although my strength is leaving me, my mind sees all too clearly the words I pass to you. Heed my words and you will become even more wealthy and powerful than I, the wealthiest and mightiest of Knights in the Court of King Richard, the Lion-Heart. The choice is yours, however to accept this challenge bears considerable hardship and danger ... both the lifeblood of a true and courageous Knight. Only the worthy may pass beyond this gate. Only the strongest will endure. To those who accept the challenge and persevere to the end, comes the promise of great wealth and honor.

Fail in this quest and you shall spend the remainder of your days rotting in mediocrity. Succeed, and your grandeur shall endure all Eternity. The choice you make is yours and yours alone. May the grace and powerful hand of God be with you in your quest.

John Holcombe

PART I
Strength, Skill and Vision

First Steps

We all come into this earthly kingdom in like manner, yet why do some prosper while others do not? And is it not also a mystery that those who prosper, often do so at their own hand? It is true, there are the fortunate few who, being born into wealth, begin the journey of life ahead of the rest. Yet victory for even those who begin a prosperous life will come only after great effort. There can be no victory without a battle! And I faced my earliest battle while still in my mother's arms.

Although we were not of nobility, we did not suffer from lack, nor did we fear from the many dangers that were common in other lands. I have but faint recollections of that special time ... a time when I had the perpetual love of my mother and the total attention of my father. How simple and special should be the life of a child! Each day, I arose to the warmth of a fire tended by a firm but loving father; living each day under his watchful eyes. Each night I fell asleep enveloped in the arms of a loving, gentle mother. Nothing on this earth is as sweet as the melody of a mother's lullaby. The lasting indelible image remaining in my mind is of my father, strong and powerful, embracing my mother in the dim hours of dawn before he rode away. That was the last time I would see my father ... the last time I would ever feel the strength of his enormous arms carrying me high above his head.

To the day of her death, my mother never told me why my father left us, where he went, or why he never returned. This was a mystery that would be solved only with the passing of years. I only knew that from that fateful day, serenity was replaced by hardship and fear. Our peaceful home in Wales had been a thatched roof cottage surrounded by tall trees and grassy meadows ... my father had been a good provider; my mother faithful and loving to us both. To them, God had given much … a first-borne son, and the promise of a second child newly conceived. But a time after my father's departure, my mother and I were forced from our home by a cruel and uncaring landlord. With only the possessions that a small ox-driven cart could hold, we left behind the only world I had known. The dangers that we would face in the dark forests were beyond my reckoning, yet I sensed my mother's fear. She was vulnerable to very real dangers being an unescorted woman with a small child at hand and carrying in her womb a second.

The thick fog of early morning lightened to reveal a forbidding path through a dense forest of tall oaks and thorny berry vines. The air was thick and moist filled with the musty smell of decaying leaves. While my mother led the slow but willing ox, I rode in the cart on bedding made of soft goose down. The cart with all it's contents were like a cave that enclosed the space all around me, leaving me with little room to move. Peeking through a narrow gap in the wood slat sides, I could see the morning dew dripping from the bushes that passed us by. The world outside was cold and damp, but in my small enclosure, I was warm … and very well hidden from view. The constant rocking of the cart and rhythmic creaking of the wooden wheels took me back to the security of my dreams. This was a magical place where I could retreat from the harshness of the unfamiliar world that now surrounded us.

I was jolted awake by the sudden stopping of the cart. Then through the slit that was my only vantage point, I saw the threatening images of several men blocking our path. My view, being very limited, prevented me from telling how many of these strangers were actually present, but I knew they must be thieves preying on the weak and defenseless who passed their way. I feared for our safety but remained silent, as I had been instructed. My mother anticipated the dangers of the trail and was prepared; the sound of iron sliding through brass resonating from her side. The subdued reflection of the morning sun glinted upon the shining surface of a double-edged sword. The men responded with loud cruel laughs, apparently amused by the sight of a pregnant woman wielding a man's weapon. With her back protected by the cart, she stood her ground as two of the marauders came at her, one from each side. I had never known my mother to be anything other than kind, soft-spoken and subservient when in my father's presence. Fear gripped my soul as I envisioned my gentle mother and I brutally ravaged by these beasts, and left along the roadside. Her voice was strong and stern as she gave the intruders warning ... I had never heard her speak with such authority. She was so close to me that I could hear her rapid breathing and see the beads of sweat dropping from her angled wrists. The men still drew closer ... then with a sudden burst of fury, the silver blade spun so rapidly in her agile hands that it appeared as a glowing blur. All around her came the sounds of the blade slicing through the air around her. A cat-like lunge to the left, another to the right ... then two men were on the ground, lifeless with bright red blood flowing freely in rivulets through the mud. All was now silent. There had been only two attackers, and their haughty laughs were forever silenced. These thieves would never return to rob and maim others who might pass this way. The sword had apparently been close at hand from the start of our journey. But, had my mother not possessed the inner strength to draw the sword and the skills to wield it against those who meant to do us harm, we would not have been spared. Otherwise, that magnificent sword along with our other few earthly possessions ... and our lives ... would have been lost to the thieves.

We completed our journey in a number of days and nights with nothing more than an occasional storm to hinder us. Our new home was to be with my grandparents on my father's side, who labored in the raising of sheep in the North Country. I do not recollect knowing my grandparents at any time beforehand, although my mother had spoken of them often. The surroundings felt strange with an air of isolation. The trees were few and the ground rocky. Instead of the sweet smell of wildflowers that grew in waves of bright colors, everything here smelled of livestock and was void of any color other than shades of brown and gray. My grandparents were even more cold and uninviting than this high country. In her youth, Grandmother had been a strong and very determined woman. She had worked alongside Grandfather in all the toils that their livelihood demanded while also raising seven healthy children. A sudden fall one icy winter caused her to suffer a near fatal injury to her head. In sparing her life, God left her totally without sight. Any other would have surrendered to death. Instead, Grandmother stubbornly held onto her life; over time honing to a fine edge the remaining senses left to her. I was terrified at first sight of her colorless unseeing eyes, her unkempt hair, and her darkened face hardened and creased from many years exposed to the elements. In time, I would find her outer appearances to be in total opposition to the beauty and kindness that was held within her. Others would have felt bitterness and hopelessness after receiving a fate such as her's. Grandmother was, instead, grateful to be alive and far from living a hopeless existence.

Her physical abilities were nothing short of amazing. From a distance, one would not notice she was without sight. She moved freely as if she saw each and every stone in her path. It was Grandmother who taught me to see with all my senses and to persist with an iron will against all adversity. I would love this ageless woman as much as I loved my own mother.

Grandfather Holcombe was a perfect companion for Grandmother. He was a massive, statuesque man of the hardiest disposition, but peaceful by nature. The pair complimented each other's weaknesses with their individual strengths. (I would learn later in my life that he had not always possessed his passive qualities.) There had never been one without the other; as children they were inseparable, as adults they were as one. They had stolen away in the darkness of a clear spring night to begin their lives together ... Grandfather at the age of seventeen years and Grandmother, then age fifteen. He remained faithfully by her side ... and she, his ... for as long as they each lived. It was from Grandfather that I learned the value of hard work, preparedness ... and the greatness of strength that comes from within. It was from both of them that I learned loyalty, for they had remained so to each other through all their challenges.

The sword, so swiftly held by my mother on our journey, was later hidden from me until years later. This, I assume, was at Grandfather's direction. The experience of that day on the path was just as confusing in my mind as many other mysterious events in my early childhood. There was so much I would never know, because my mother died a few short months later giving birth to my sister. Only through the wisdom of my grandparents and a lifelong search for *Truth*, have I been able to gather together the many fragments of my earliest childhood. The death of my mother thus ended my life as a helpless infant and began a new and long journey marked in the beginning by toil and adversity, followed by learning and ingenuity; ultimately bring forth fruit beyond my grandest expectations.

◆ ◆ ◆

We are all born as equals. Life begins the same way for everyone, whether they be privileged or poor. If we are granted our first breath, we are not certain how many more will follow … if any. As infants, we have few choices but we also are responsible to no one. We cannot choose the family or surroundings in which to begin our lives, yet why do so many blame their heritage as their excuse for failure? A knight has but one acceptable answer for failure: "I did not do what was required to succeed. I blame none other than myself for my failures and my weaknesses."

When my father and mother were taken from me at such an early age, I was not aware of such things as wealth, success, social standing, and the like. As a very small child, it was only important to have sustenance, warmth, and love. For those fleeting and wonderful years, I was totally dependent upon my father and mother. Later (and even more so), I looked to Grandfather and Grandmother to teach me the wisdom of their years and to help me become strong and independent.

My sister was to become my confidant; the one with whom I could always share my deepest thoughts and feelings. All that I am, I owe to those who gave me counsel, beginning with my grandparents. It was only after possessing the skills so uniquely theirs that I later ventured away from familiar surroundings to the outer kingdoms.

Seeing Without Sight

My greatest marvel was Grandmother's almost mystical abilities. My sister and I would try, unsuccessfully, to take advantage of her blindness through harmless pranks. However, it was not possible to hide from her or to be in her presence without her knowledge. At an early age I was curious and prone to exploration. I held deep inside of me a desire to see places and things that I had not seen before … to explore and experience the unknown. In the far distance was the highest of hilltops; a place well outside the realm of my permissible boundaries. It was on a clear mid-afternoon that I set out on my own to see what lie beyond that vantage point. A gentle wind rustled the few clumps of grass left behind by the ever-foraging sheep. I left the immediate company of my grandparents (as I often was prone to do) and believed my disappearance would go unnoticed (which it did for some time). The excitement of discovering something new radiated from within me. By my side I felt the warmth of our shepherding dog, Lanny; he was always my constant companion. I reached the hill's crest to view the far-reaching vistas while the shadows had grown only slightly past their midday size. How quickly the hours pass when one is absorbed in matters of deep thought. I did not realize the full extent of my troubles until the familiar forms of trees and hedges dissolved entirely into the shadows. It had become futile to walk about, as I could not so much as discern the path beneath my feet or the obstacles that lay alongside of it. This I discovered very painfully when I tripped over a large stone and landed face-first into a thorn bush. Once free of the entanglement, I could only sit in the darkness not knowing the extent of my injury. After a considerable lapse of time, I heard from the far distance, the beautiful sound of Grandmother's voice calling my name. I was certain my cries back to her were lost in the wind, and after a time I could no longer hear her calling to me. The feeling of loneliness was eased only by the warmth of Lanny lying with his head in my lap.

Grandmother's movement through the night was both effortless and silent. I didn't hear her approach and was quite startled when I found her sitting by my side. She knew every stone along this well-traveled path, as this hilltop was her special place. This was where she came to be with the Creator when her earthly life grew too difficult. In time, this too, would become my special place where I would often bare my soul to God. Long after she had departed this world to be with her Lord, I would follow her path ... the path of truth and courage.

For several hours longer we stayed, all the while Grandmother pointing out the many things I had not noticed before ... the sounds of a ewe calling her lamb ... the smell of smoke from a distant fire ... the feel of the wind brushing against my cheek and flowing through my hair. Every sensation was amplified through the mind's-eye of Grandmother. Then when it was time to return, she softly took my hand and showed me how to see without eyes. These talents would later serve me well on the field of battle, as I could strike a fatal blow under the cloak of darkness without my adversary ever sensing my presence!

The punishment I justly deserved that night never came. I had learned a very painful lesson on the hilltop and would not be so anxious to repeat the experience very soon. But Grandmother was a willing guide and teacher, so the next evening we began my training. We would travel throughout the countryside, navigating the most hazardous of terrain, such as the steep and slippery hill where I had first become lost. Once I had gained the confidence of Grandmother to safely navigate the dangerous outer boundaries ... day or night ... then I received the gift of freedom to go and come as I chose. And from Grandmother, I also received the greatest gift of all ... the gift of insight. Through our many walks together, she shared the following secrets with me:

Look past that which only your eyes can see and feel the presence of everything around you.

While I was still a very young child, she would cover my eyes, allowing me to see the world around us as she did. I was amazed that she never confused her days from her nights, yet there was no apparent way for her to know. She gained a keen sense of time, committing to habit those things that must occur each day. If you always arise at a set time, you do not need the sun to know night from day. She also knew the signs that precede the dawn. Since the darkest hour of the night is just before the dawning of a new day, this is the coldest of all the hours. It is the hour that sounds of the night are stilled and sounds of the day commence. The owls cease their mournful calling; the crickets and frogs lower their voices; while the birds of the day take to flight. On several early mornings before sunrise, we left the warmth of our home to walk a long distance into a hidden meadow. There we sat among the wildflowers and grass ... so uncommon for this desolate country. As the sun began to glow brighter over the distant horizon, I felt the morning chill followed by the moisture of the dew. In the moments just before the appearance of the sun's first rays, a dead silence would fall all around us. As the morning sunlight fell upon the dew-covered meadow, millions-upon-millions of tiny leaves raised their heads toward the east in an enthusiastic and deafening applause. The air permeated with the fresh sweet smell of wildflowers opening their blossoms for the world to see. And we became as the flowers, lifting our faces to the sun to feel the warmth upon our cheeks!

It was not enough to simply observe. Grandmother required that I be able to recognize even the smallest particle of my environment through any one of the senses. She taught that the only ones truly blind are those who do not see the world around them. In time, I developed a keen awareness of my surroundings. Like Grandmother, I developed the sense of premonition. By understanding the precise nature of things, one can predict an event before it happens. Is not the coming of winter always preceded by fall? Are not the rains preceded by the shading of the sun? All living beings follow a pattern that has been repeated since the beginning of time. Study the habits and nature of all that is around you and you will gain the gift of premonition. Study the habits and nature of people and you will understand their hearts.

Learn to use all of your senses to the fullest.

Extend your hands and you feel with the tips of your fingers. Extend your mind and every part of you has feeling. When I was lost on the hilltop, I did not hear Grandmother's approach. She felt the ground beneath her through the bottoms of her feet, walking ever so lightly to find her way. The very hairs on her arms told her when a bush or tree limb was close by. Once you perceive a presence, you might use your hands to define shapes and texture. But if you use your mind, you learn to perceive even the presence of God!

How is it possible that a ewe is able to find her lambs among all the others? To man, all sheep look and smell alike, but that is because it is not important for us to distinguish the looks or smell of one sheep from another. For the ewe, it is most important. Everything has an odor unique unto itself. Grandmother knew her way on the trail from the familiar smells of those things along the way … the smoke from the house in the next valley, the sheep in the meadow beyond the second hill, the different flowers and trees in their unique place … and finally, she found me from the odor of the dog by my side. It was through smell that she also recognized something clean from something soiled, or food that was no longer fit to eat. How much more meaningful is a flower when you not only see the enticing colors of the bloom, but also feel the softness of the petals and smell the sweet fragrance as well. How beautiful appears the bride who is outwardly beautiful like a flower … even more so if these qualities come from her heart. Outward appearances are but a facade. Always look beyond appearances to fully know the most subtle and hidden qualities of something ... or some-one.

We are surrounded by sounds we do not hear, although we are not deaf. Is it because we do not notice or because we do not care? *Neither reason is acceptable!* Open your mind to the sounds that saturate the air. Do you hear the songbird joyfully singing his melody? Do you hear the leaves of the trees rustling in the wind? Do you hear the voices of those around you? More importantly, do you sense the meaning of their words? Be silent and listen!

Sweet ... bitter ... sour; these are the sensations of taste. Does this not also describe how we feel and act? Just as one can sense these quali-ties in something by taste, you can also sense in others the sweetness, bitterness, or soured feelings found in their hearts. A knight must know what is in someone's heart ... taste the fear, the anger, the love. But more importantly, know what is in your own heart. The feelings you hold inside, even though they cannot be seen by others, are felt through their other senses. Condition your heart, as you want others to perceive you. If you want to receive the hate of others, feel hatred towards *them* in your own heart. But if you want to be loved by all, then hold the love of all humanity inside of you. Just as a knight in bat-tle attracts the fury of his enemies, a knight that shows kindness in times of peace, is repaid with equal or greater kindness from those who would be his friends. The knight who holds confidence in his heart on the battlefield and love in his heart in quiet familiar surroundings will live a long and peaceful life. No so to those who always garner hatred!

◆　　◆　　◆

The most important lesson I learned from Grandmother is one she did not include in her tutoring. I learned that nothing need be a barrier to one's achievement. Grandmother had every right to be bitter towards her blindness. She could have spent the rest of her days sitting alone in a dark cottage depending upon others for sustenance. Instead, she chose to be free of her affliction the only way that she could. Grandfather shared with me the difficulties she endured while over-coming her lack of sight. At first, she was dependent on others to care for her. She began with a simple routine … always arising at the same time each day, always retiring at the same time each night. Just as my boundaries had been confined as a child, her's were also very limited. Once she could move freely inside her home, she widened her circle ever larger to include the outside until she was no longer bound by the familiar. Throughout her life, she would always extend her reach past what she believed possible, and in so doing, she was able to accomplish the impossible. So it is with us. If we would only stretch our capabilities further than we believe possible, we too, will achieve great things.

Hardship: Gaining the Strength and Courage of a Warrior

G randfather was a soft-spoken man of boundless strength. When I was a small child, he appeared to me as a giant (as he did to most everyone else). Each day he arose early to prepare for the heaviest of work that would carry him past the setting sun. In all of the days I knew him, he never complained or raised his voice in anger. He lived a simple and peaceful life that was lacking in possessions, but abundant in many other rewards. It wasn't until much later that I learned of another side to Grandfather … a side that was far from peaceful and content. When I had just passed into manhood at the age of 15, I was not only small in comparison to Grandfather, I was small compared to others my age. I have no explanation for my lack of size, as I was in good health and received ample nourishment. I was also accustomed to working by taking care of tasks that required considerable walking … except I usually ran instead.

Throughout humanity, there are those who, being stronger than the rest, choose to inflict harm upon those who are weaker. Such was my experience on one misty day while I was retrieving a number of yearling lambs that had strayed a great distance from the flock. I was returning to our meadow when a man and three large boys blocked my path. I did not know any of them, as they were from another place distant. The largest one of the three boys threw me to the ground while the other two beat me until I was unconscious. The man simply looked on silently with a look of amusement across his face. When I awoke, it was approaching darkness yet I could plainly see that neither the marauders nor our lambs were anywhere near me.

19

Each step I took on my return homeward was a painful struggle. My face and head were terribly bruised; my eyes swollen nearly shut. I felt a dizziness that was totally foreign to me, causing a terrible wrenching in my stomach and dropping me to my knees. The journey homeward took untold hours at my feeble pace ... once there and safely inside, all went black as I fell to the stone floor in total exhaustion. To the best of my ability, hours later, I explained what had happened to Grandfather. In silence and seemingly without emotion, he momentarily retreated outside, returning shortly with a long, fleece-covered object. From within the covering, he withdrew a magnificent sword of glistening steel with a shank of finely woven leather. Into the night he disappeared. When he had not returned by the next morning, I feared he had been injured or killed by the thieves. Grandmother, who should have shown far more concern than I, appeared as if nothing were out of the ordinary. When I questioned Grandmother, asking her why she did not show any distress over Grandfather's prolonged absence, she touched my hand and bade me to sit quietly. She then told me something about Grandfather that I would not have known otherwise.

◆   ◆   ◆

Many years earlier when Grandfather was a young man eager to conquer the world, he was befriended by another young man who, unbeknownst to Grandfather was the heir to the crown. Their chance meeting occurred when the Prince had strayed into the countryside and had become accosted by bandits. Grandfather ... tall with broad shoulders and arms like the limbs of a mighty oak tree ... easily dispersed the attackers. The Prince stayed awhile afterwards with Grandfather, but never revealed his true identity during that time. Several weeks after the Prince had returned to his home, Grandfather was summoned to the King's Court. Hearing of Grandfather's heroic act, the King enlisted Grandfather as a royal guard to always accompany the Prince wherever he went (in case the Prince was inclined to wander, he would, at least be protected by someone that could be trusted). In his early years, he was taught all manner of skills in defense by the noblest warriors in the land. His perpetual presence with the Prince afforded him, by default, the same education that was administered to the King's son. My grandfather would ultimately become the mightiest and best educated of all the men in the King's service.

Grandfather remained in the service of the crown for some time after having wedded Grandmother and started a family. By then, the Prince had become King. Grandfather's life was constantly interrupted by the demands of service to his king. His life as a guardian of the King would offer him fame, wealth, and glory, but would deprive him of the time he longed to spend with his family. When all the battles had been fought and won, he chose to leave the King's service and seek a quiet life in the Welch countryside.

When my father was a small child and grandmother still had her sight, grandfather was called back into the king's service for yet another quest. This was the second and final time he would fight in England's bloody battles. All those earlier years of fighting as a master swordsman had taken its toll, so when he had faithfully completed his first years of obligation to the king, he sought peace in this quiet distant place. But he would not be allowed to enjoy the serenity for long. England entered yet another war; leading to more bloody battles ... the king would request his service a second time. It was while he was away that grandmother had the accident that took away her sight. Were it not for my father coming to her aid, grandmother might have died of her injuries. This time when Grandfather returned home, he vowed he would never leave his wife and children again ... he would never fight in another war. As a warrior, he was the most feared of all the king's soldiers. Had he remained in the king's service, he was assured to gain a sizable fortune. Instead, he chose a humble life of solitude with his family over the fame and fortune of knighthood. Although he could have had great honor and wealth, he exchanged it all in return for tranquility. To be certain he would never again be tempted to fight,

Grandfather changed his identity and disappeared into the highlands where he remained until his death. In time, I too would face the same decisions … only then would I truly understand.

As evening faded into the second night, Grandfather reappeared with our lambs. There was no need to ask what had happened, the traces of dried blood on his clothing revealed all that was necessary to know. Neither Grandfather nor Grandmother would speak about the incident … it was not important how the sheep were regained, it was far more important that I was ill-prepared to defend myself in the face of adversity. My grandparents realized that I was not equipped to survive in the world beyond our meadow, and that the time was quickly approaching when I must face that world alone. It was time now for my physical and mental training to begin.

◆   ◆   ◆

Through the rough hands and soft words of Grandfather, I learned how to be strong and fearless so that I might overcome whatever might befall me. Grandfather was the master of overcoming adversity, so this was a subject he could teach with unquestionable authority. While the bruises were still dark on my face and body, we began my training. On the first morning, as was always his habit, Grandfather arose early to start his day. Up until then, I did not know what he did in those early morning hours before beginning the work outside. Today I would know. Today, I would be under his constant watch and instruction. Through his instruction, I would gain not only physical strength, but I would also discover truths only revealed to the most educated in the land. These are the greatest of these truths:

> *Do not begin the efforts of a single day without preparation. Time is very precious and to expend your energy on tasks not clearly thought out is a waste of your time.*

Each moment of the day should be planned and each task ordered according to their proper importance. Grandfather awakened me from my slumber to share the most important time of his day with me. Before he began his work, he planned. Before he planned, he kneeled in the quiet darkness of the cottage to seek the guidance and strength of Almighty God. This day we prayed together, as we would do every day until my time with him and Grandmother was completed. Grandfather looked to God for physical and inner strength to overcome the challenges that we were not able to handle on our own accord. This we did aloud. We then sat silently before the fireplace; just a dim glow remaining from the dying embers of the night before. In this time of total solitude, we allowed our minds to see what could be … not just for that day, but for weeks, months, years … a lifetime to come. In the darkness of those precious moments, I saw my future unfold in my imagination. In those visions, I was a strong and mighty knight. The battles I would wage in my thoughts would always end in glorious victory … I would be honored by my countrymen for my bravery … my wealth would multiply beyond what I could ever believe possible. And with God as my strength I knew *all* things were possible.

Once Grandfather had laid out the day in his mind, we would begin his tasks only after he had shared his thoughts with me. At first I obediently listened, but as I grew older, I was expected to share in the decisions. We planned how we would conquer the work of the day. His ultimate task was to build a small frail boy into a skilled warrior … an undertaking that would take three grueling years to accomplish.

A knight must be strong to overcome adversity; however one only becomes strong <u>by</u> overcoming adversity.

This is one of life's magnificent contradictions. As an infant, were we not faced with overwhelming obstacles and few abilities? We could only lie in the position and in the spot where others had placed us. But we could cry when we needed (or wanted) our mother's aid, and we could move ever so slightly. As we continued to cry and move, we grew stronger ... we would kick our legs a little harder ... we would expand our lungs further. Our endurance and strength would grow, as we grew in size. Eventually we could turn our heads, then roll over from one side to the other. Rolling over led to sitting up. Sitting up led to crawling ... to standing ... to walking ... to climbing ... to running.

So what is the solution to this ancient puzzle? Persistence! To become stronger, we must work our muscles ... and our minds ... to their limits and beyond! When we reach what we believe to be the extent of our abilities, we must persist until we break through the barriers that hold us back. Then once one barrier has been broken, we must constantly strive to penetrate the next. Once we cease this process, our growth ceases ... we not only stop our ascent to greater heights, we begin a decline that ultimately ends in our deaths. Never cease your quest to grow ... persist and live a long rewarding life!

Grandfather was strong because he never ceased a daily regimen of hard physical labor. He was wise because he never ceased to learn.

> *Skills are best learned by doing ... they are mastered by doing them repeatedly.*

Grandfather was a master swordsman. In battle, he instinctively moved as if the sword was a part of him. This skill did not come to him quickly or with ease. It required hours upon hours of effort. Once his training had commenced, he was bound to an oath of commitment to never let a day go past without practicing his art. Had he not upheld his oath, he might have paid the price with his life. Once you have made an oath of commitment, master your new talents and practice them as if your life depended upon it!

Success in any endeavor, I would find, was solely the result of habit. Grandfather was quick to point out that this was true for both good endeavors and bad, however the rewards of good endeavors were infinite, as were the penalties for bad ones! Choose your talents and endeavors wisely; learn the skills you must have to become a master; then make it a habit to repeatedly practice your skills.

Just as skills are formed through repetition, excellence in those skills comes from focusing one's attention solely on the task at hand.

Grandfather had many amazing abilities, but one that I found most unusual was his ability to perform many tasks exceptionally well. The very cottage that he shared with Grandmother was built by his own hands from stone, wood, and thatch found nearby. He was equally skilled in the raising of sheep ... yet he was highly educated and skilled as a swordsman. While possessing all of these talents and sometimes having a number of activities occurring simultaneously, he was most skilled at limiting the number of tasks to only what he could successfully handle while setting a level of importance for each ... then *focusing his attention* on that which was most important at the time.

One can never succeed by doing too many things at once. However one may accomplish many things that exist at the same time by doing only what is within one's reach and tending entirely to each in their order of importance. It was not necessary for Grandfather to concern himself with the raising of sheep when they were contentedly grazing in the meadow. He could continue to raise sheep and still accomplish many other things. If the cold of winter was approaching, he would not give up his raising of sheep to devote his energies to digging ample supplies of peat to fuel the fireplace. Once a task was begun, he would not cease unless something of more importance arose ... such as the birthing of a lamb ... but once the urgency had been dealt with, he would return to the former task until it was finished.

Finishing his tasks was all-important. Not a single task, did he begin, lest he saw in his mind the final acceptable conclusion. Thus he would focus all his energies and attention on the immediate task until it was accomplished before beginning another. Accomplish all of your tasks by focusing your attention on the most important one and in all of your endeavors, seek excellence as the only acceptable conclusion!

*Just as a fire cannot burn without fuel, a knight cannot be strong
to endure the battles without taking in ample foods of substance.*

From our land, we grew and gathered all that we needed for nourishment, but the rewards did not come easily. I moved rocks of enormous size to uncover small patches of tillable soil. I found my appetite
becoming insatiable, and as our garden became larger, so did our rock
wall ... and so did I. At first, I didn't notice the subtle changes occurring in my appearance. I only felt the pain that comes from long grueling hours of backbreaking effort. After a while, the pain would subside
and the work become easier. Grandfather, sensing I had grown accustomed to the demands on my slight frame, would then demand heavier
loads and less rest. All the while, I was allowed to feast on a variety of
fresh vegetables grown in our garden, fowl that we captured from the
fields and fish caught from the streams. At the end of three years, I was
moving boulders effortlessly, and had grown into a near reflection of
Grandfather.

Although I ate in ample quantities, it was never to excess, nor was it
ever in absence of strenuous physical effort. The work at the hand of
Grandfather and the meals by Grandmother's, took me from being a
small frail boy to a mountain of a man. Remember that life requires
tremendous effort to be fulfilling. The weak can only ponder what the
strong can easily accomplish! To be strong, a knight must work hard,
eat properly and keep the two in balance at all times. To be strong is a
long and difficult challenge, but the rewards are great and never-ending
... choose to be strong!

◆   ◆   ◆

Each day would end as it began ... on our knees in the presence of
God. At this sacred time, we thanked Him for the help only He could
give for the day's efforts. Our time was always well spent and eventually, all that I dreamed of would become reality. Through Him all
things ARE possible. He is an infinite source of strength and wisdom.

Three years from the beginning of Grandfather's instruction, God had molded a fragile boy of 15 into a tower of strength. For so long as I lived, I would not cease the struggle, for to do so would ultimately shorten what precious time I had left while I lived. To God give thanks for the struggles that life brings you, for it is those struggles that make us strong and give us a life worth living. Amen.

Beginning the Journey to Knighthood

I believed truth and courage to be all-important. Without these, there can be no victory over struggle. To know the truth is absolute before one can act; to act decisively one must have the courage to do so. Armed with the truth of my purpose, the courage to seek it out, and the sword of my father, my struggle and quest to gain knighthood was soon to begin. This was to be my destiny and my dream ... both of which were inspired by my greatest mentor, my grandfather. As I reflect upon this time in my life, I must ask, "Why is it that so many have the desire to do great things, yet so few succeed?" The answer, I have come to conclude lies in one's lofty expectations of what is possible and total dedication to reach what one knows to be possible. Most, truly want the best life can offer, but how many are willing to pay the price? I dare say very few. My sons and daughters, remember this:

> *There is absolutely nothing that separates the elite from the paupers EXCEPT their expectations.*

If you wish to rise above the masses, you must know in your heart that it is possible, then let the fire burn fiercely within you. Do this, and *IT SHALL BE DONE!!*

Each moment of each day, I saw the vision of myself in my mind as a courageous knight suited for battle atop a beautiful and powerful stead. My ultimate purpose ... my dream ... was to earn a place among the brotherhood of the king's knights, then live the glorious and honored life of adventure with the rich life that would surely follow. As a continual reminder, I carried with me always, a small scroll of sheep-skin, with the words I would someday emblazon on my crest. Those words were: *Veritas et Fortitudo*, which means "Truth and Courage". These are the words I have lived by. These are the words that I will be remembered by on my crypt. These are the words that are your heritage my sons and daughters!

When the day soon came for me to say farewell to Grandfather and Grandmother, I was prepared. From them, I had learned the basic skills to not only survive, but to overcome adversity. They had taught me the skills to succeed and helped me to grow strong and powerful. Today began a new and exciting adventure that would be marked by great adversity and danger ... and sadness. Grandfather's final act was to deliver to me the sword of my father, who before me and like his father before him, had also been a mighty knight; one who fought valiantly but died in battle without sharing his knowledge with his only offspring. The sword bearing the inscribed name "Holcombe", was to be the golden key allowing me to enter the gilded doors of the King's Court. Once inside, I must stand upon my own merit to enter the King's service. Remember my sons and daughters:

Each of you, too, must stand on your own merit. The name of your family may open doors to opportunity, but you, and you alone, must walk over the threshold and put forth the effort. You cannot ... you shall not receive one farthing from my labors ... you must succeed by your hand alone. What I will not give you in gold and silver, I give freely of my knowledge. This is much more valuable and will endure throughout the generations. It will set you free!

The journey begins ...

◆   ◆   ◆

My travels after departing the lands I had known from infancy, took me over vast distances. The stark rocky landscape of the high country gave way to lush green meadows and dark forests. Many small peasant villages crossed my path, with great distances in-between where I would not encounter another soul for days. I allowed my mind to wander in these lonely times of solitude, thinking frequently of the beloved family I left behind. Grandfather and Grandmother were nearing life's end, while my sister … now a beautiful young woman … would soon desire her own freedom. Like my father and I, she grew up learning the skills of survival. Until those skills would be needed, she would remain with our grandparents throughout their final days.

As I drew further from familiar country, I could not allow my attention to waver; with each step towards London, my awareness of the surroundings keenly increased. At night, I would rest but sleep little; always on guard for the unexpected. It is written in God's great book to walk in faith. One cannot spend a lifetime worrying about what "**might**" happen. To quote Grandmother, "Don't concern yourself with what **might** happen. A 'mite' is a very small creature. Walk always in faith, but do so with your eyes open wide!"

During the day, I met few traveling the paths and roadways; whenever I did, I was watched with suspicion. In all cases, other travelers appeared in groups of three or four. They undoubtedly considered me a fool to make such a treacherous journey alone. Some would see me as easy prey to rob and leave dying by the wayside. Not all who passed me by would have the good sense to keep walking. After many days of travel near dusk, I was approached by three men who looked and smelled of questionable character. Their words were few but their eyes told much. Tonight, I must be on alert, for the strangers would surely linger nearby.

The fire I prepared was not for warmth, but was instead a stage set for any who meant to do me harm. From my surroundings, I fashioned a human likeness from stones, sticks, leaves, and moist earth that I then covered with my bedding. Secretly in the shadows I would lay in hiding, prepared for any unwelcome visitors. There would be no fire or blanket near me tonight to stave off the cold damp air. I saw nothing in the heavy darkness, but I sensed the movement of everything. In the nearby leaves came the rustling of a mouse in search of a morsel. The unexpected movement immediately drew my attention. Above was the sound of the wings of an owl soaring above the treetops. The flowing of air through feathers grew increasingly more pronounced, followed by an intense but short-lived struggle; the mouse, gripped securely in the owl's talons. Stretching it's powerful wings, the owl reversed it's descent … as quickly as it had descended from above, disappearing into the night's dark sky. There shall always be these life and death struggles between the strong and the weak. Life is filled with silent dangers, so be certain you are among the strong! Unlike the tiny mouse, this night I would not be easy prey.

My suspicions were confirmed in the late night hours. My fire was still alive, casting a yellowish glow upon the underbrush nearby … enough to betray it's location, but not sufficient to illuminate but a few feet from it's core. The disgusting smell of my would-be attackers arrived far ahead of them. I lay in wait, following their every step with the inner vision of my mind. With my Excalibur drawn and ready, my breathing was slow, controlled, and silent. The trio sprang from the darkness in a flurry, pounding my likeness with wooden staves. The illusion of my likeness was evidently sufficient to convince them it was real, as they chose not to survey the bludgeoned mass beneath my blanket. Thinking I was dead, they pilfered through the few belongings I had purposely left behind then made their escape back to their camp some distance away. Although I was incensed by their assault, I remained in hiding, following closely and silently behind. So long as they believed me to be dead, I held the advantage.

The cold became more intense as the night grew on, and soon, their fire would demand more fuel. When the first ventured away from the security of their camp to retrieve sticks, I swiftly yet ever so silently liberated the dog of his head. This one never once sensed my presence. While his head rolled down the slope, his torso remained standing momentarily as if uncertain what to do next. Reaching forward, I grasped the outer garment, and gently lowered it to the ground.

The second intruder, apparently annoyed by the deepening cold and the slow return of his companion, came in search, only to meet his death in the same manner as the first. As I lowered the second body to it's resting-place, I sensed a presence from behind. Without the slightest hesitation, I swung my blade around catching the final thief squarely through the chest, but not before his blade had sliced a direct blow to my right side. I could contain the bleeding, but without aid, I would be in danger of fever and infection. Upon further inspection, I found two ribs to be cut halfway through. Tonight I must rest, but tomorrow, I would seek aid … a forbidding task in a land of strangers. For now, I would face another challenge. Without shelter or a fire, the cold of the early morning hours would penetrate my injured body all the way to my soul. Within a few hundred paces away was my intruders dying fire, and at my feet lay the sticks collected by the first of my three assailants. With great effort, I blocked the intense pain from my thoughts and collected much of the fuel into a single bundle. This would be sufficient to sustain the flames until sunrise.

The fire took little encouragement to regain its former intensity. A few small sticks followed by several very thick ones, and it was now possible for me to rest and soak in the fire's warmth. As I drifted in and out of consciousness, I thought about the chill of night and how it was much like the cold, harsh and uncaring world I had entered. Up until this point in my life, I had had little contact with people outside of my beloved family. In all cases since beginning this journey to the outside, I had found people to be cold, uncaring, and certainly not to be trusted. Where would I find kindness among so much adversity? The answer came from Grandmother's teaching:

"Whenever you find yourself lacking either in ability or knowledge, your solutions are only as far away as a prayer ... no matter what trials you face, give them up to God." With these words heavy on my mind, and the ache gnawing in my side, I drifted off to sleep.

◆   ◆   ◆

This night I had faced death and survived. This would not be the last time I must choose between my life or the life of another human being. However, the taking of a life ... even of someone who threatens yours and provokes your wrath ... will burden your soul throughout the remainder of your life. This was the first time that I had taken the life of another; I could not shake this thought from my mind, even in my sleep. All of the years of my training had made my movements instinctive, but the act of actually killing another had caused me to pause just for an instant while fending off the last of the intruders. That slight hesitation was all that was needed for him to strike his damaging blow. I would never again hesitate when my life or another's was at stake.

My dreams turned to nightmares as I envisioned the demons of hell forcibly taking me into a burning lake of fire where I would be tortured for my transgressions. I struggled to overcome their hold on me, but could not; the fumes of burning sulfur filled my nostrils and singed my eyes. I cried out for mercy but to no avail ... they forced me to the edge of a precipice and threw me head first into the churning red cauldron below. I felt myself falling downward, spinning in an ever-increasing spiral ... my face and chest throbbing from the intense heat radiating off my body. The pain was so severe, I wished I could die, but then I realized I must already be dead. One final scream before plunging into the fiery sea ... then abruptly I awakened, with sweat dripping profusely from my face.

While in my irrational state from a great loss of blood, a gust of wind had fanned the flames of the fire ever higher and hotter. The intensity of the fire had added to the realism of the nightmare. As I cleared my thoughts, backing away from the flames, I found myself again in the presence of the demons, only I was not dreaming! Terror ran through me like a sharp spear ... I must be dead and I am, indeed, doomed to die in hell! The figures grew nearer from all sides and clasped me tightly, bringing me to my feet. The sudden movement caused the throb in my side to erupt into a violent agonizing explosion of pain. At that point, I completely passed out ... darkness and a deafening silence enveloped me.

PART II

Loyalty, Love and Wisdom

At the Hands of Others

I could not know that, while I remained unconscious, these silent captors intended my death. I was entirely at the mercy of these strangers ... and like all the other strangers that had passed my way, sought only to do me harm. Grandfather warned me of the perils I would face in this inhospitable land, and I believed myself adequately prepared. But despite my precautions, I now was facing death at the hands of these people whom I knew nothing about. Even if I were not in this weakened state, there were far too many to ward off. For a brief moment, my vision cleared only long enough to see the swarm of angry men hovering over me. At that fleeting instant of clarity, I prayed for God to free me from this certain death. I could not die ... not now ... not before I had fulfilled my destiny! Then, as if the hand of God had fallen upon me, my field of vision collapsed again into total darkness ... the angry voices becoming muffled and distant.

When I again opened my eyes, I had a total feeling of peace. My body felt as if it was floating and I felt no sensation of pain. As I was able to see more clearly, I saw a bloody figure lying on the ground illuminated by a multitude of blazing torches. Surrounding the body was an angry mob of men ... enormous shadows of their silhouettes spreading into the darkness beyond. Some carried clubs, some had objects used for farming, others carried torches. Their angry voices filled the air, then ever so slowly, I drifted upward and away into the silent tranquility of the heavens. The noises became fainter as the images grew smaller; then shortly, a mist of white vapor enveloped me. Everything around my being was absorbed into the clouds until I could no longer see anything, although my eyes were still open. When the mist faded away, I found myself standing at the entrance of a very long dark cavern, with a single shaft of light shining from within. I approached the strange light, cautiously at first, then at a more trusting pace. As I drew nearer to the light, it grew in both size and intensity, until it's glow was almost blinding. As I reached the end of the cavern, I felt the warmth of the light inviting me to venture outside. Behind me was only the cold darkness. Coming through the mysterious light was a man and woman walking hand in hand who were dressed in pure white. The intensity of the light made them difficult to discern at first, but as they drew nearer to me, I recognized them to be my father and mother! Joy overcame me. It had been so long since I had shared their warm and loving embrace, I wanted desperately to do so now … I could not. I could go no further than to the caverns mouth.

My father and mother came to within a few paces and spoke to me. First my mother:

"It is not your time. You may only stay with us for a while then you must return. You have much you must still learn and much you must accomplish. You were reared in isolation and do not yet understand people. At this moment, you believe the world to be filled with uncaring self-serving people. You must seek out the good in people and you will find the world to be a much better place.

Your purpose, John, is to become a great leader. To become a great leader of people, you must first serve them; to serve them, you must love them; to love them, you must know them; to know them, you must seek them out; to find them, you must gain their trust; you must be trusted <u>first</u> before they can trust you. Then and only then will you understand their hearts to know how best to serve them. Do these things with all your heart and with sincerity, and people will trust you, seek you, honor you, love you, and serve you with undying loyalty."

Then my father:

"I was taken from you before I could share the knowledge and skills that are required of a knight. Your grandparents have given you much, but you have learned very little of what is necessary. Now you must go back into the world and continue your journey without my hand or the hands of your grandparents to lead you. Your mother has just given you clues to the mysteries of success. Now, you must find the answers on your own. And my son, you have yet to know the questions! Have great courage, my son, and seek the truth. God will be with you always."

I had so much I wanted to ask, but I was totally immobile. I could neither move nor speak. I could only stand silently and listen to my father and mother's words. In a deafening rush of wind like none other, the light … and my parents … disappeared, and all became dark.

To Trust, Seek, Honor, Love and Serve

The blackness faded to a light gray, but I was unable to see. I no longer felt the stony ground beneath me, nor did I hear the voices of angry men wishing to do me harm. Peace surrounded me; the chill of the night air was gone, and I could smell the unfamiliar aroma of fresh pork roasting on an oak fire. My skin was damp from perspiration and the pain in my side had subsided to a dull throb. I knew I was alive, but I did not know how or where. When I tried to move, I felt soft fingertips caress my cheek and a woman's gentle voice bading me to lie still. She removed a damp cloth from over my forehead and eyes, allowing me to see my surroundings. I was in a small room of modest appointments, a fire burning on one side in a stone enclosure. Standing over me was an angel with long flowing brown hair, fair skin, and dark green eyes. Her smile was warm and reassuring. An older woman stood near the flame tending to the sizzling meat suspended over the flame, while two small boys raced through the door from outside. A giant of a man followed through the door behind them. The sight of him brought fear to my heart, but I remembered vividly the vision I had had of my parents and their promise that God will always be with me. I followed the man's every movement with my eyes, daring not to move. As he drew nearer, a smile came across his face ... his huge hands resting lightly on my forehead. "The fever is all gone" says he, "You've done good, daughter. He'll surely live til the morrow."

I could only ask myself, "What then ... do I meet with a tortuous death at the hands of these and many other angry peasants?"

This man's smile told me I was in a safe place for now and was free to rest without worry. There were so many unanswered questions running through my mind. Where was I? Who were these people? How did I get here? And the one question I feared asking ... What did they intend to do to me? The answers were soon forthcoming.

No angry mob came that day, or any other day. My angel, I learned, was a girl named Dora. All the while I was mending, she was at my side giving me a spoonful of porridge, a piece of bread, or a drink of water. When I was not in need of nourishment, she was tending to my wounds.

In a few days, I would be strong enough to sit on the edge of my new bed and eat and drink on my own. Dora was always nearby to render assistance, even though it was no longer necessary. For the brief times she was absent, I quickly grew impatient for her return. Through Dora, I learned that the felons that I had disposed of had been terrorizing the local inhabitants for quite some time. The loud and unruly crowd that I had encountered was searching for my attackers, and upon finding me by their fire, had mistakenly thought I, too, was a member of that murderous trio. My life was spared when their bodies were found in the woods nearby. My wounds would confirm the farmers' theory that I was intended to be the next victim. It appears I had accomplished the bloody task they had set out to do themselves. I was near death by the time they were able to render me aid, and would not have lived through the night had they not appeared to me when they did.

The people here were simple peasant families, preferring to live in peace. I saw what they could do if provoked, but now, they greeted me as if I was royalty. They showed me a kindness I had not experienced from strangers since my journey began. In the months to follow, I would come to love this people as family ... especially would I love one very beautiful young woman with long flowing brown hair, fair skin and dark green eyes.

Each day I grew stronger, and when my wounds and broken bones had fully healed, I sought out all those who had delivered me from the hands of death. I worked in their fields, I gathered their wood, I did all manner of physical labor to show them how much their kindness meant to me. The hard physical effort helped me to regain my strength and become even stronger than before. By working and living alongside these grateful families, I learned much by listening to their stories. They told of hard times and good times, of the changing seasons and their hopes for those yet to come. They shared interesting and delightful accounts of their lives, and all I had to do to get them to enrich me with their hopes, dreams, and life experiences was to simply ask them to tell of themselves ... then listen with great interest. It seemed so illogical that they should be so open with me, but then, before they would share their deepest feelings, they had to trust me as a friend. I gained their trust by being sincere in my dealings with them. I gave of myself, and asked for nothing in return. The more I gave to them, the more they gave back!

It was, at first difficult for me to venture past the walls of my new home to face the others. With Dora's encouragement, I took walks with her to meet the other families. Dora told me about each family, and how important their names meant to them. I found them to be kind and trusting when I addressed them by name. Remembering who they were and what their names represented showed them considerable honor. I became very dear to these people; they showered me with their love (and many wonderful meals!). How strange it seemed that I knew so much about them, yet they knew so little about me! This paradox is one, my sons and daughters, you must remember:

It is far more important for you to know about the lives, hopes, dreams and feelings of others than for them to hear you speak these things of yourself! Strive always to encourage others to talk freely about themselves. You will know that you are following this principle, if you know much about many people, but few know but little about you!

The Lasting Chain of Friendship

Among the families, I grew especially close to five other young men who were about my age: Edward, George, and Daniel, and two brothers, Bruce and Randall. There was much we had in common but even more that we could share and learn from one another.

Edward was a quiet one who took much abuse from the others because of his awkward, spindly frame, but otherwise had a kind and compassionate soul. He was the most difficult to know because the others made him feel as if he was an unworthy companion. He was, in fact, the one who taught me the most important lesson of all. From Edward, I learned that everyone has great value and has much worth sharing. He had very special gifts as a hunter and in the raising of animals. Through him, I learned the secrets of stealth and entrapment ... skills invaluable to a knight. Edward chose not to lead others. Instead, he was content living each day surrounded by his family and reaping the rewards of his daily toil. His days were marked by familiar tasks repeated over and over again ... he thrived on stability. It was through the familiar and unchanging tasks from one day to the next that gave him contentment. I never once knew Edward to get angry or upset. He would live a long life ... his final days identical in routine to those of his youth.

My sons and daughters, know and remember that not all people are destined to be great leaders or achievers. Do not look down upon them for choosing a life that to you, appears dull and mundane. It is far better for one to be a worker than a beggar or thief! Respect those who toil and are happy doing so. These are the ones who make up the masses and without them, there would be few followers. Also remember that achievement takes many forms and for some, it appears as creations of beauty that can be seen or heard rather than appear in the form of great possessions or position. These people show their joy by loving others. If in no other way, be like the Edwards of the world by seeking contentment from your lives and by sharing your love.

George was resourceful and ambitious. Of all my new friends, he carried himself with the most confidence and charisma. He knew how to lead instinctively, and could demand more effort from others than what seemed humanly possible. Through him, I acquired many secrets of leadership. I also learned how to work hard and long to the point of utter exhaustion, then extend ones reach even further through sheer willpower. He possessed the gift of enterprise, the knowledge of numbers and the special skills essential to acquire great wealth. George and a pair of workers could accomplish more in a day than ten others could accomplish in a week. George, however, was a harsh taskmaster. He drove people long and hard and had little sympathy for those who were too weak to keep up. While under his control, workers gave more; but few would remain as his followers. George, in time, would live a lonely life with few friends except for his ever-present flask of wine. Such is the life of this kind of leader … one who drives people like a herdsman drives his cattle then falls to the lowest of depths when failure eventually overtakes him.

My sons and daughters, a knight must demand the efforts of his followers only when dire circumstances warrant. When those circumstances arise, he must be certain his followers understand why extraordinary effort is absolutely essential. Followers can understand the need to give more of their labors if they understand the reasons. At all other times, a true knight commands the efforts of his followers through persuasion. He first instructs how the tasks are to be accomplished, allows his followers to "learn by doing" under his watchful eye, then leaves them on their own to do what was instructed. Upon their completing what was asked of them, the knight rewards excellence for all to hear; he corrects poor performance privately, but always with encouragement. People will do great things when they have the desire; they will only do what they are commanded to do if the desire is possessed only by a taskmaster. The followers of a true knight are many and they follow out of loyalty and respect; they thrive on recognition and rejoice when given ample commendation that is justly deserved ... they are remorseful when their efforts are not met with approval. A knight's followers are very proud to be serving under his leadership and will serve a true knight unto their deaths! They would rather die than lose their knight's confidence.

Daniel was an intellect. He had acquired the gifts of reading and writing through the teachings of an old yet scholarly friar. Through Daniel, we all gained the ability to read and understand the written word and to speak silently through the use of words scribed on scrolls of leather. We also learned how to approach problems in a logical manner. These skills, over time, would open our minds to the knowledge of the ages. By reading the works of great people, one learns the secrets of becoming great. What Daniel possessed in intelligence and logic, he lacked in ambition. He was content to spend his days learning rather than doing. In time, he would live a pauper's life with a multitude of great ideas locked inside his mind.

My sons and daughters, always remember that learning unlocks the secrets of the universe, but you must apply your newly gained knowledge for it to be of value. If you will seek the wisdom of those who have gone before you and apply the knowledge you have gained, you will achieve great things. It is said one learns by making mistakes ... it is far better to learn from the mistakes of others. Remember that great people are known by their accomplishments and for sharing what they have learned with others. Always learn, never stop feeding your mind; but learn NOT merely to gain knowledge ... learn so that you can do! Then do great things and share the knowledge of your achievement so others can learn from your successes ...

and your failures. Only through applying knowledge can you truly become wise!

Bruce and Randall were like James and John, Disciples of Jesus, the Christ. The Biblical James and John were also known as "the Sons of Thunder." Like the two Disciples, Bruce and Randall had a knack for finding trouble. They also were as big and as strong as oxen, so they feared nothing that came their way. Of all of my adopted brothers, Bruce and Randall were the most like real brothers to me. It was one of their many contradictions ... they would ceaselessly intimidate those who showed cowardice towards them, but would befriend with undying loyalty those who stood up to them. Once you were in their inner circle, you were there forever. Thus it was also with me when I first met with their acquaintance.

One evening after my wounds had sufficiently healed, I was sharing a peaceful stroll with Dora. Our path took us along the steep banks of a deep but gentle stream (and far away from the watchful eyes of her father). It was one of many quiet moments we would share in the days and weeks to come. But on this occasion, the peace would come to an abrupt end with Bruce and Randall solidly blocking our way. Although they were much larger than myself, I showed little if any fear of them. It was not my desire to engage in combat so soon after getting back on my feet, but these "Sons of Thunder" intended otherwise. When I refused to back down from them, they lowered their heads and came at me like young bulls. With a slight shift of my weight in rhythm with their forward momentum, I handily diverted them both headfirst into the stream. Their confidence instantly melted after they entered the water as neither knew how to swim! As they thrashed their arms and begged for help, I saw no alternative but to dive in after them. It had been far easier throwing them into the stream than it was getting them out! I all but had to drown them myself to get them to stop resisting. Randall was the first to be extracted followed by Bruce. We must have appeared a noble sight ... the three of us lying exhausted on the muddy bank opposite to the one where Dora now stood laughing at us all. From that day forward, I was Bruce and Randall's closest companion … making it very difficult for Dora and I to share but a few rare private moments together afterwards.

Once the brothers had taken me into their confidence, they taught me the secrets of their great physical strength. It was their great size and bulging muscles that gave them such confidence. This was also what made them win the frequent battles that seemed to come their way. Their secrets were simple ones: plenty of heavy physical labor, plenty of food, plenty of rest, and very few worries. When the day came for me to leave my adopted family and close friends behind, it would be Bruce and Randall who would be at my side through the journey that lie ahead. I knew they could bravely face danger and would never tire or weaken. Any task they <u>chose</u> to assume (as no one dared force them into a task!) would succeed either by skill or through brute force. If they couldn't open a door, they would go through it! Bruce and Randall enjoyed life and living, and I loved them because they were exciting to be with. They were also deeply loved by their comrades because they actually possessed huge giving hearts … another contradiction. Much of their labor was freely given to others, more often for a meal than for gold. In time, one would join the ranks of knights and rise high above the masses, the other would succeed in other ways. They would not live privileged lives as did the Lords, but they would live lives that were greatly enriched.

My sons and daughters, if nothing else I've said remains in your thoughts, remember this! One who has great possessions without happiness is a pauper compared to he who owns little but lives a fulfilling life. If you must choose between the two, choose to live a life filled with joy and excitement, and share it with others. However, great wealth achieved with joy and excitement can be the grandest of all ways to live. The secret of enrichment is measured more by what you give than what you have. If you have much, give much, and you will be both rich, and enriched!

I knew I could not stay in this special place forever, and it was soon time for me to continue my journey. My dream, my vision was to become a knight for the king, and to achieve this meant doing whatever was necessary … wherever it was necessary for me to go. I was driven by this singular purpose. Once I had achieved knighthood, I thought it might be possible to return. I would find that over time I would change and grow while people and surroundings here would not. I would never cease my love for these strong yet caring people of this quiet setting, but there would be many others who would also command my love and attention. A knight, by his very nature, is the servant of all the people, and must be shared. Followers and acquaintances outside the brotherhood of knights are many, friends few. And precious little time is shared with family … those who love and need the knight's attention the most.

My deepest regret, my son's and daughters, is that I could not have been with you and your adoring mother more. When I chose to pursue knighthood, I accepted the sacrifices that followed. I did not realize the sacrifices would come at such a high price. In my final moments, I see all too clearly how little of my time and knowledge I've shared with you over your lifetimes. My only hope and my prayer in my final hours is that you can know me better through these Testaments I share with you now. It is too late to share with you otherwise. I painfully realize that my words cannot begin to fill the space in your hearts that should be filled with warm memories of our times together. Please forgive, understand, and at all cost, give the best of yourselves to your families.

Nearly two years would pass when it came time for me to continue my journey. Dora and I felt a love for each other that was more special than words could describe and leaving her behind was the most painful memory of that time and place. She was my first love but I was not sure if she was the one God intended for me to take as my wife. If it were meant to be, it would come at another time. This day, I would leave

Dora behind to pursue my destiny. For just a short time, she was in my presence; she would forever be in my dreams.

I would think often of my experiences here and wonder what fate awaited my many friends. Edward, I knew, would always go about his labors with a huge smile on his face, and for good reason. He was the only one of us that was content with his life.

George would possess much land and cattle, but would live alone in his grand home. Every day would end in a drunken stupor; his final days marked by poor health and bitterness.

Daniel departed briefly to study the works of great philosophers. Upon his return, he would marry a very plain but hard working woman who earned a few farthings washing the clothes of the nobles. She would be their sole source of income as Daniel would spend all of his days immersed in thought, while consuming large quantities of roast pork. His death would come suddenly in his sleep from gluttony.

With the brothers, Bruce and Randall, by my side, we continued on the path to our hoped-for destiny as knights. Our lives, from that moment on, would be filled with adventure, excitement, and at times, terror!

PART III
The Path of the Valiant

A New Adventure

A rmed with new skills, much larger physical size and greater strength, Bruce, Randall, and I ventured onward. It had been two long years since I had left the high country. I knew that as my grandparents grew older, they would be well taken care of by my sister. Regardless, I longed to be with them once more. A few weeks backtracking would be inconsequential compared to a quest of a lifetime. As our travels brought us nearer to sheep country, I began to recognize the familiar landmarks. This was such desolate and isolated country with few people and a multitude of stone. The long and familiar path soon appeared that would lead us to our destination. It was a long meandering trail that crossed several small streams before winding in a circular fashion ever higher along the hillsides. This was a place that no one would find without someone leading him. Near the path's end was the most barren and isolated of places on the face of the earth. My family's home, made of the same kind of stone that dotted the hillsides, appeared out of place in this vast emptiness. The sheep that once roamed these hills in search of the sparse forage had been sold long ago just before my departure. Our sheepdog, Lannie, having died while I was still a young boy, appeared reincarnated at the front of the house. After vigorously warning the household of our arrival, this new dog kept his distance but never let us out of his sight. I felt a strange cold fall over me as I drew near the entrance. I would have expected a greeting long before now. Upon further inspection, I found no one to be at home, although there was noticeable evidence that someone was still living there. We had no choice but to wait for my family to return. We knew not if this would be a few hours, or several days.

Shortly after nightfall, my sister and Grandmother appeared from out of the shadows. There was still no sign of Grandfather. They appeared much relieved and surprised to find me waiting by the door. Surprise turned to joy and tears. Unknown to me, Grandfather had died suddenly within a few months of my departure. As I was too far on my way to be located, it was not possible for word of my grandfather's death to reach me. My sister had, as was expected, cared for our grandmother (even though Grandmother was very independent and capable of doing quite well without assistance). But problems of another sort had appeared within recent months. Fugitives from the king's dungeons had fled into the high country to avoid capture and execution. They found this desolate and sparsely populated sheep country to be an ideal place to find refuge. At first they could move cautiously from place-to-place, just stealing whatever food and belongings they might need. As their stay became more permanent, they grew bolder in their ways. Instead of covertly taking what they could find, they now approached homes during daylight hours and demanded whatever they wanted. Now that they had seen my sister, the danger to her was much greater than the loss of food or belongings.

Upon my arrival to the cottage, the two women believed the three of us to be the thieves and had fled to one of several well-hidden caves. Whenever the intruders had come by in the past, they would rummage around the home place, take what they wanted, then leave when it was apparent my sister would not be coming back. Grandmother and my sister would always wait until after dark to return … Grandmother was well equipped to walk the treacherous pathways at night, but the intruders were not. The fugitives, by necessity, had to leave well before the sunset.

I now understood why my sister and grandmother had been startled to find us at their door. Now that they were here and telling me all that had happened in my absence, the deluge of unhappy news was almost too much for me to bear. The pain of losing Grandfather turned to guilt for having left them for such selfish reasons. Grandmother, always so wise (and always outspoken) eased the hurt I was feeling inside. She told me that:

Today is for the living. Tomorrow is just a promise. Yesterday is but a memory. We must all do for today, because we have lost yesterday's opportunities and tomorrow may never come. It was a bittersweet consolation. Grandfather was the greatest man I had ever known or ever expected to know ... I would always miss him dearly.

I learned that up until recent times, the fugitives had not ventured often to our home because it was so distant from the main byways. It was a difficult trek and once at the house, the takings were light. The only prize now worth their trouble was my sister and the pleasures they envisioned having with her.

Listen well, my daughters, never take lightly the dangers that are always present around you. You are valuable beyond anything that can be bought or sold ... you are a priceless treasure! Always know your surroundings and your companions; be vigilant of the risks and avoid them. My sons, you must be your sisters' protectors until they have found security in families of their own. Watch over them and guard them against anyone or anything that might do them harm.

I felt as if I had betrayed my sister by leaving her to face these dangers. But again, I believed Grandfather to be in good health, and I knew him to be a formidable challenger for any intruder. I thanked God that Grandmother and my sister were still safe, although living in fear. I learned there were an untold number of the fugitives traveling in a band, but apparently no more than six. It was time their thievery came to an end, but not knowing their where-abouts, we decided to wait for them to return. Grandmother and my sister would go to a cave at the first sign of their approach, while Bruce, Randall, and I would secretly lay in waiting where the intruders would not suspect our presence. When the thieves made their way back to their place of refuge, we would follow a safe distance behind. Until we knew where they were hiding and how many there were of them, it was not prudent to attack prematurely. Ultimately, we held the advantage, as they would not expect us, nor would they be a match for our strength and skills. Over the past several years, Bruce, Randall, and I shared countless hours honing our fighting skills. They were excellent in hand-to-hand encounters, while I was a master with the sword. By sharing our knowledge of combat, we would all become masters at both methods of doing battle.

Several days passed uneventfully, with nothing more than an occasional sparrow to break the monotony. Before our arrival, the women had been forced to go without a fire for heat or for cooking to lessen the chance of attracting attention. Smoke drifting across the sky would have certainly been noticed by the unwelcome intruders. Our intention now was to do exactly that. There was a bumper crop of hares to supply our table along with fresh greens, so we ate our fill while we waited, watched, and listened for the approach of strangers. As we had anticipated, a pair of strangers happened by to investigate our activity; their approach far from discrete. One of the great advantages of living in high places is the superb vantage point for detecting visitors early on. There was ample time for Grandmother and Sis to reach the cave long before our unwelcome guests had made with their arrival. My friends and I quickly and quietly moved to a spot that had to be several hundred paces away from the house. Just exactly as was described of their appearance, a pair of dirty, unshaven men slight of stature appeared at our door and entered without the slightest hesitation. I could see Randall's face growing a deep red from anger … he had left a tasty meal behind that was now being eaten by the thieves. By every indication, only my sister and grandmother had been in the house as the stage had been carefully set to appear as if only two people had been there. It was now up to the uninvited guests to eat their fill and return to their sleeping place with their comrades.

They were not difficult to follow. They weren't the least bit wary, while on the other hand, we moved down the path silently with great agility. They led us to an obscure path that followed a small running stream. It was near dark when they reached their destination; a thatched cottage hidden deeply in a thicket of high bushes. We watched as two more men appeared at the cottage door. Nightfall that particular night was especially dark, as there was no moon and heavy clouds obstructed the stars. We were well adept to moving in the dark, but the fugitives would be totally blind without the sun. It appeared almost too easy. We would simply set the house ablaze and take them as they stumbled into the night. This plan did not prove possible, as the house was occupied by not only six fugitives, but they were holding the family hostage that lived there as well. Burning down the house could prove fatal to the innocent family. A better plan had to be devised.

The fire inside made the house glow a pale yellow, giving off sufficient light to reveal everyone's position inside. Bruce, the taller of the two brothers, hoisted me onto his shoulders while Randall handed me a bundle of rags he had placed onto the fork of a long stick. I was not altogether certain where the chimney opening was, but I could tell if I was drawing closer by the smell of smoke. When I believed the rags to be directly over the chimney opening, I gave the stick a determined jerk, and the rags fell directly into the mouth of the chimney and lodged, securely plugging the opening. As according to our plan, the cottage quickly filled with smoke driving everyone outside, where we were waiting. It was not difficult to tell the innocent from the guilty. The family (father, mother, and four small children), concerned about each other's safety, banded together in a small group in a safe area away from what they thought was their burning home. The others were only concerned about themselves and dispersed singularly in many directions. Amidst the confusion we so quickly and effectively took the fugitives to their deaths, not one of them realized they were under siege!

With the last one face down on the ground, and dead, the family assured us there were no more. We then hurriedly extracted the bundle of rags from the chimney before it could catch fire, and sat with the family outside as we waited for the smoke to clear. This home had been occupied by its unwelcome guests for several months, while the family was forced to care and feed for these violent fugitives. During their stay (which so abruptly ended), the six visitors had been anything but congenial with their hosts. It was then we learned that the band of thieves had planned to move to another location. Their choice was our stone cottage tucked far away from any passers by. God had delivered these men into our hands at the best possible time and place. Another day would have been too late for my sister and grandmother … they would have either fallen prey to these ruthless travelers, or have gone cold and homeless.

We chose to return to the cottage during the hours of darkness so Grandmother and Sis would know it was us returning. As for the family we had liberated, they had no regrets dealing with the six corpses lying about their home. They would tend to cleaning up after us.

The return to my home was much easier than we had expected it to be as the clouds had cleared away to allow our pathway to be well lighted by the stars. It would be another frigid night, but this night, families throughout the region would sleep warmly. All would soon hear how the fugitives met their ends, but for now, Bruce, Randall, and I were content knowing that justice had been served.

A true knight is strong and defends the weak, asking nothing in return. His is a life of abundant honor, yet he neither seeks honor nor does he expect it. A true knight is forever humble, bringing him even more adoration. Thus another magnificent contradiction: he who seeks honor or praise receives neither, while he who gives of himself freely and seeks no reward receives a never-ending supply.

It had been a very long and tiring night with little rest and little to eat. Awaiting us that night was a warm cottage and a hot meal. Before taking our places around the table we gave thanks to God for helping us through this dangerous challenge. To God I gave a silent prayer of thanks for the strength he had given us and for taking away the guilt I had felt for leaving Grandmother and Sis without a protector. *Today was for the living. Tomorrow … just a promise. Yesterday … but a memory. We did all we could do for today, because we lost yesterday's opportunities and tomorrow may never come. But if it does, we will rejoice and use each precious moment wisely!*

Difficult Choices and Fleeting Opportunities

We felt no urgency to remain now that my family was safe. But what about next week? Next month? Next year? I could not leave Grandmother and Sis alone without an assurance that they would be safe. At the time of my first departure, I left with the peace of mind that Grandfather would be there to protect them. In my immaturity, I assumed that Grandfather and Grandmother would always be there ... that they would endure and remain as I had known them. How foolish and so very thoughtless I had been. Grandmother, now sensing my uncertainty, allayed my concerns with her beautiful wisdom. She reminded me of advice she had given to me such a long time before, "Whenever you find yourself lacking either in ability or knowledge, your solutions are only as far away as a prayer ... no matter what trials you face, give them up to God."

My answers would be found in deep thought and meditation in that special hilltop place where I had strayed as a young child. In the darkness of night, I made my way up the narrow path with great ease. I thought back on that small child lost in the darkness on this very path ... Grandmother had taught me well in the ways of the blind. In that familiar place of solitude, other images of my past reappeared before me. The familiar sounds and smells of the country I had come to love (and now deeply missed) enveloped me. The deep realization that Grandfather, so strong, so wise, was no longer among us came over me like an arrow through my heart. I have learned in my latter years that a deep loss of a loved one does not quickly strike your heart. While enraptured with the challenges of defending the lives of others, I had not considered my own loss. Now that I was isolated from all other concerns, my grandfather's image came to me in a vivid memory. That quiet yet immensely wise mentor would never again give me counsel to guide me into the unknown. In the emptiness of my surroundings, I wept bitterly over his loss while allowing my thoughts to drift freely like the clouds now floating eerily across the face of the moon. I then remembered Grandmother's favorite saying, "Don't concern yourself with what might happen. A 'mite' is a very small creature. Walk always in faith, but do so with your eyes open wide!"

My sons and daughters. You will always be faced with challenges that at times appear unconquerable. Always remember that we are but mortal men and women and do not have the privilege of knowing what lies in the future. You cannot prepare for everything that you might encounter, and to even attempt to do so will cause you much grief and waste of precious time. Do not concern yourself with things that "might" happen ... most of your worries will never appear. Those events that will happen will, most likely, do so despite anything you may do to prevent them. That is not to say you should not prepare for the inevitable. One can expect with surety that night follows day, so you know to gather fuel for your fire while the sun is still shining. Take the needed action to prepare for those events that will certainly occur. For those things that may never occur, prepare by remaining strong, always gaining in your knowledge and skills, then "walk always in faith, but do so with your eyes open wide!". And, when your abilities are inadequate to overcome what lies before you, then seek out a place of solitude and allow the wisdom of God to guide you and His strength to carry the burden that you cannot.

The answers to my questions were well beyond my knowledge, skills, and strength to solve, so I surrendered by soul and gave it all up to God. After considerable thought and prayer, I chose to stay with grandmother and my sister for a while; I could certainly postpone my ambitions for a few weeks. Besides, Bruce and Randall did not appear to be in any hurry to leave ... so long as the supply of hares was plentiful.

There was much that needed attention ... repairs to be made, fuel to be gathered, food to be stored. With Bruce and Randall's help, much was accomplished in a very short time. But after a while, I thought Bruce was acting rather peculiar. Whenever we were out in the hills working, he appeared distant. I feared he was either ill or in some way disheartened by our change of plans. When we were all together in the cottage, he would act foolish and child-like. My sister also began acting quite unlike herself. Randall and I found their behavior quite curious. Grandmother would only smile.

A month or so after we eliminated the fugitives, we were visited by mounted soldiers of the king's army. It seems they had been searching all of England for the thieves. Upon learning we had ridded the kingdom of the menace, they sought us out for a first-hand accounting. The soldiers encouraged us to journey with them to London and present the details in person. Randall readily agreed, but I was hesitant to leave the women alone, even though the threat was not as great as before. In reality, we had little choice in the matter. To my surprise, Bruce suggested he remain behind to watch over Grandmother and Sis, so that Randall and I could go to London with the soldiers. This was acceptable to the soldiers and a relief to me ... Bruce would vigilantly look after my family. A few days later, it occurred to me that no one was at my home to look after Bruce! The eventual marriage of Bruce and my sister some months later came as no surprise. God could not have delivered a better husband or protector for my family. God had also answered my prayers and provided solutions that I could never have acquired on my own.

Listen my sons and daughters to this truth. All things are possible with God's help. Also know that you must patiently wait for God's answers to appear to you. We pray in our time ... God answers in His. His answers may never come in our lifetimes, but the answers will come at the right time!

Even though the soldiers were no longer needed for their original purpose, they were always on alert for any disturbances that might arise. Randall and I were perfectly adept to walking, however the pace of the horsemen was often quite rapid. We had no idea that news of our short-lived battle was traveling ahead of us at a pace much faster than that of the horsemen. We also could not have known how exaggerated the event became as it was retold. Upon reaching a small village a few days travel south and eastward, we were met by a small crowd of twenty or so locals. We were cheered and congratulated for confronting an army of ten Scottish highlanders who had been conducting raids on small northern villages. As we drew nearer to London, the size of the crowds and of our exploits grew accordingly. Upon reaching London, the numbers of people lining the roadways were beyond calculation ... Randall and I just marched on in disbelief of the reception we encountered. One would have thought we single-handedly fought off an invasion of all England!

With little in the way of money, we were not expecting much for accommodations. At best, we had hoped to stay in the stable with the king's horses. Instead, our escorts arranged our quarters with them, along with food and bath. In all the excitement, we had not bothered to ask to whom we would be giving our report. For myself, I thought it would be one of the many scribes of the king. At the appointed time, we were shocked to find ourselves bowing before the king's throne. We were giving our account to King Richard himself!

"Am I to understand the two of you single-handedly stopped the invasion of 200 Nordic Vikings? Is it also true you were armed only with stone axes and sheep shearing knives?"

As much as I would have wanted to perpetuate the myth, I thought it prudent to be totally honest, especially since the penalty for lying to the king was certain death. Randall and I shared the stage as we gave the truthful accounting of our experience. Of how we had banded together with Bruce beforehand with intentions of traveling to London to seek places in the king's army, but delayed our departure to return to my home in the high country. We concluded with the factual accounting of finding Grandmother and my sister living in fear of the thieves and finally of our liberation of the area from the six fugitives.

Upon hearing our factual account, the king then informed us that he had already verified the incident as it actually happened, and found the truth to be extraordinary in itself. He commended us for our heroic efforts and of our truthfulness in accurately reporting the event. He then granted us each a place on the palace guard ... an honor reserved for only the most loyal, trusted, and skilled warriors in the kingdom. An honor that would be ours ... if we were able to prove ourselves in open competition against the best swordsmen in the kingdom. We would face this challenge individually; one, both, or neither of us would win the competition. We would have seven days to prepare.

Know this my sons and daughters. I had spent a lifetime preparing for this event. This was my dream ... my sole purpose for existing. I was ready at that very moment; a week would have made no difference. When the opportunity arose, I clearly saw it as such. Without a dream or a purpose, I would not have been prepared to seize the opportunity once it arose, nor would I have known that the opportunity was, in fact, there for the taking! If you know the "why" of your efforts, the "how" will be self-evident! Dare to dream great deeds and take action to seize your opportunities when they assuredly appear.

Through our many great times together since we first became bonded as brothers, Randall had adopted my dream as his own. Although Randall had not received the intense years of training as I from my grandparents, I had enthusiastically shared my knowledge and skills with him. I seriously doubt that my best friend would have even considered the pursuit of knighthood, if it were not for my enthusiasm.

All the persuasion in the world would not have convinced him to join forces with me without my abundant enthusiasm and sincere belief.

Randall, too, was prepared. If allowed to fight together, we could have fought all of the king's best all at once and won just on the tremendous energy we held for our dream!

For the seven days allotted to us, we were granted a comfortable place to sleep, plenty of good food to eat, and an area free of distraction where the two of us could practice our craft in private. During that time, we had no contact with the world outside the castle gates. Had we taken the time to wander about and see all of the new and strange surroundings of London, we would not have held our focus.

My sons and daughters beware! The world is overflowing with distractions that rob you of your time, energy, and focus. One must continually guard against these things or else forever lose your sense of direction amongst all the chaos.

Our skills as swordsmen, already unsurpassed, became even sharper through intense practice. On the day of our trials, we were unstoppable. Although we were fitted for armor, we chose not to use it, as we were not accustomed to the added weight. Our opponents would be in full metal coverings from the tops of their heads to the end of their toes. I suppose in retrospect, being exposed as we were could have been very dangerous. *However, it would have been more dangerous to change a system that worked very well for us.* Our decision proved to be a wise one.

It was difficult for me to sleep on the night prior to our trials. Not so for Randall. He slept so soundly, I wasn't sure he would awaken in time for his match. We were given very little information about the event, except that we must meet many challengers and if successful, we would be inducted into the king's elite palace guard … the personal protectors of the king and his family. These special champions are the best in the land and must be prepared to die if necessary so harm did not come to the royal family. Upon successfully beating the challengers, the best would still have to meet with the king's approval. On many previous trials, we were told, contenders having superb abilities were denied their prize because they lacked the character that befitted the duty. The ones ultimately chosen possessed standards of conduct of the highest magnitude. They, at all times, placed the well being of others ahead of their own. Thus a paradox:

You must want to be one of the chosen few to an extreme, or else you would not take such dangerous risks, however you will be denied your dream if it must be achieved at the expense of others ... including a dream you treasure as much as life itself! Know the difference between being a keen competitor and being ruthless. Listen to me now, my sons and daughters. Look closely at what motivates you. If your success must come only by cheating others, you do not deserve the prize and will ultimately be denied it! If you gain your success while always placing the good of others ahead of your own, your achievements will come to you even greater than you had envisioned and all will share in the jubilation!

Of those chosen, the king would someday knight a very elite few for extraordinary acts of courage. To become a knight was my ultimate dream; winning today was absolutely essential to even someday be considered for knighthood. In too many cases, those knighted achieved their success posthumously! My dream was to achieve knighthood, but I was not in any hurry to die ... if there be a choice. If chosen for the king's guard, I would serve to the death if necessary, but I would continually improve upon my abilities so that death would not come prematurely.

My sons and daughters, risks are inevitable as is death. Never assume a risk that might take your life unless the cause is a worthy one. And what are worthy causes? Your God, your family, your country ... in that order! There is nothing as senseless as one who dies needlessly either through carelessness or stupidity! You have but one life ... use it wisely. And may you live one that is long and prosperous!

At the appointed time of the competition, we were brought into a very large room with stone floor and walls, and a very high ceiling. There were no windows; the only source of light being torches along the walls. A large assembly of competitors and members of the king's guard were already in the room when we arrived with our escorts. The sheer number of contenders took me aback. Most, if not all, were professional soldiers in the king's army who, for various reasons of their own, were compelled to match their skills against the rest. Some simply wanted to prove their skills, others desired the great honor, some competed from sheer ignorance. It was here in this musty smelling room that we learned what we must do:

We would first draw lots from an equal number of short and long straws. Randall and I both drew short straws (an omen that made us both feel somewhat uneasy). After having drawn our straws, all of the competitors would reassemble in a competition area some distance away. All those with long straws would select an opponent with a short straw. The custom for those with long straws, we learned, was to try to choose the smallest opponent possible to increase ones chances. Neither Randall nor I were small, but neither were any of our opponents.

After pairing, all competitors would be given a signal to begin, at which time all competing pairs would fight simultaneously. This would be an initial elimination. We were to avoid bloodshed … if at all possible. A victor of a match would be declared when either one of the two conceded defeat or if, in the opinion of official observers, an entrant's defeat was without question (this only occurred when one of the opponents was on the ground, no longer in a position to defend himself, and is a strike away from certain death).

With the formalities out of the way, I had a passing concern over the likelihood that these competitors had abilities superior to mine. These were the best in the land with years of experience in matters of combat. I decided, however, that the king's best were soon to be soundly embarrassed.

I would not allow self-doubt deny me of my dream! My sons and daughters, the battle is first won in your own minds. The reward of victory comes only to those who believe they are worthy. Believe! Then decide you will not be denied your dreams!

As we filed from the room, we found we were nowhere near the place chosen for the competition. We were led through the castle gates, then through the streets, which, to our amazement, were overflowing with commoners and peasants. A huge crowd followed behind us as we led the way. People from throughout the kingdom had come to see the two peasant boys from the high country vie for a place in the king's guard. Never in the history of these events had the number of spectators been so large. The whole affair was almost more than I was prepared for. How could I possibly hold my attention on my opponent with so many people watching my every move?

An area sufficiently large enough to hold all of us was cordoned off from the swarm of people. Overlooking the "field of battle" on a raised platform sat the royal family and high-ranking members of the king's court. After some light formalities, we were paired with our opponents to await the king's order to begin. Facing me was a giant of a man who stood head and shoulders taller than I; a deep scar following the curve of his left cheek. The number of marks and creases on his breastplate were reminders of many fierce battles from times past. I was facing a veteran of many battles. Randall fared no better. In reality, we were the most feared of all the competitors ... only the king's fiercest soldiers were willing to match their skills against ours.

The two of us were the only ones without the protection of a coat of armor. At the sound of a trumpet's blast, the crowd ceased their milling about. A few words from the king was followed by a moment of absolute silence as an official of the games perched high above the warriors held a banner high above his head. A slight tip of the king's hand and the banner fell forward, stopping at the railing with a loud crack.

The silence instantly turned into a flurry of arms and swords swinging wildly within a giant circle of yelling, screaming on-watchers.

Instantly, I centered all my attention on the man before me. Where he held the advantage in size and in the protection of heavy armor, I was much faster and more maneuverable. Each time he drew down with his sword, he would find that I had vanished from his view. Rather than try to match his strengths, I took full advantage of mine. I moved so rapidly, that I could respond with two or three solid strikes to each one of his attempts. This was becoming quite enjoyable. Not so for the other fellow; the heat inside of his armor must have been unbearable. He soon tired and was quite easy to topple with a slight kick from behind. Forward he fell in a clang of tin and brass. Once down, I held the tip of my sword to the base of his neck, ending any thoughts of a final skirmish on the ground. The observer declared me the victor of my match; likewise Randall easily won his. The next round would not be as easy.

This event would be the ultimate test. All those who were not eliminated in the first event were reassembled in the field of battle. At the king's signal, it was every man for himself. Unlike before, we were being attacked from every direction at once. Instinctively, Randall and I paired, as we had so many times before. Back to back, we fought our attackers off as they tried in vain to catch us off guard. At first the others were battling those around them in a hit-or-miss fashion. They would swing to one on their right, then their left, then around to one behind. A few fell away early on and were removed from the circle. As the fight continued, Randall and I became the target of every competitor remaining. Many were stunned when our blades penetrated their armor and drew blood. Even though none were seriously injured, some bowed out because they imagined their wounds to be much worse than they actually were. Others quit in anticipation of wounds that might actually be more severe.

My sons and daughters, there are many who will conjure up any excuse for quitting. Some reasons based on a real concern ... others imagined. In reality, they never possessed the burning desire to overcome all adversity to win the prize. Only a rare few will ever achieve their dreams … only a rarer few will ever possess dreams worthy of achievement!

In the final moments of combat, it came down to the two of us against six of them. For a short instant, our attackers stopped outside the range of our swords apparently to take a momentary rest. We could hear them gasping for each breath of air inside their closed helmets. Trails of sweat leaked down the front of their breastplates in steady streams. In contrast, Randall and I could feel a cool gentle breeze flowing around us. We had fought defensively to that point, but held plenty of energy in reserve. At the moment of their inactivity, Randall turned slightly and gave me a subtle nod. In a sudden tempest of slashes and hacks, we downed all those left standing. In the end, it was just the two of us, but there must be one more contest. Randall and I would be required to face each other in a fight to the end; only one could remain. Only one would be chosen as champion!

This was not the victory I had imagined. We were now placed in opposition to one another. The noise from the masses was horrendous as we faced each other for the final trial. For Randall's ears only, I told him that this was not right … I would not fight a brother! He silently agreed with another nod; we then faced the king, bowed, and drove our swords squarely into the ground at the same time … a sign of surrender. I had lived and breathed every moment for this opportunity, and in one single instant, I had given it all away. I chose Randall's friendship over the dream I had prepared my entire life for.

This now presented the king with a problem; there were no more contestants from which to select a champion! This had never happened before, and it caused quite a stir among the crowd. It was the king's final proclamation that Randall and I both would be declared equal victors! We would share the honor and both enter the inner circle of the king's royal guard. We had passed the ultimate test of integrity by choosing friendship above our personal wants and desires. We would both enter the king's service on a journey that would eventually take us to strange and distant lands at the ends of the earth. Our dreams were coming true before our very eyes, and would bring us great fame, fortune, and ultimately, knighthood.

The Secrets of Wealth

The years to follow in the king's service would be filled with experiences one could not even imagine ... some uneventful and rather dull ... some exciting to the point of sheer terror. Our duty for the king required us to constantly train and prepare. In time, Randall and I would become as skilled in armor as we were without. We would also learn such things as strategy and tactics; we would learn to be experts in the art of war. We would also find in our travels throughout the land that there was much we had never seen and had no knowledge of. I had on many occasions the opportunity to escort noblemen who were close associates of the king court. These were men who had achieved great success in other ways; men of influence and great wealth. I was exposed to the trappings of the elite ... fine horses, the most beautifully crafted carriages, sprawling estates with the grandest of homes filled with treasures from strange and distant lands. In my youth, I had no wealth but it did not matter, as I had no knowledge of the things I was without.

I did not know what I did not know! Such is the state in which most commoners exist. Our experiences horribly limit our expectations, and we achieve no more than what we believe exists to achieve. If we want little, we gain little ... likewise, if our expectations are small, so will be our achievements! My sons and daughters, strive to see and experience all that is grand in the world and learn to have grand expectations of what life can bring ... then go forth and achieve great things.

Absolutely the most dramatic effect my new role would have on my life, would be to open my eyes to what the world had to offer. As I became more aware of the privileged lives lived by noblemen, I was at first curious how they were able to obtain such great wealth. If you have lived your life in a world far removed from those of great means, you assume they are wealthy because they have always been so. It became very apparent that this was not the case. Wealth can be achieved by anyone who learns the principles and is willing to apply them. Once I realized that it was just as possible for me, a peasant, to also gain great wealth, I possessed an unquenchable thirst to find the knowledge.

Hear me my sons and daughters. If you have the desire to succeed, whether that be to gain great fame or accumulate great wealth, you must learn all that is possible from those who have reached the level of success you want to achieve. Do this by watching what they do, and do the same. If they are willing to teach you, fasten yourself onto their coattails with a death grip and never let go. You may find great companionship among your equals, but you can never learn the secrets of success from them. They simply do not understand ... if they did, they too would possess great fame, position and wealth! Always seek the advice and counsel of those who have proven they understand what is required for success. In the very likely event you cannot find one willing to teach you their secrets, glean through any and all writings either by them or about them; some, if not all of their principles will be revealed to you. As you learn more and apply what you have learned, a mentor will present himself to you when you are ready!

Such was my great opportunity. Randall and I had become quite well known throughout the land from our success in the competition. Once the door to the king's castle opened to us, other doors opened in-turn. One such door was to the home of Mr. Bertram Smythe, London's wealthiest wool merchant. To those who knew him well, he was simply, Bert. After all the years of seeing, eating, working, and smelling sheep in the high country, it was difficult for me to associate that very ignorant animal with great wealth. This is because I did not possess the knowledge needed to open my eyes to this incredible opportunity, even though the opportunity had been before me in abundance.

Be aware, my sons and daughters, opportunities surround us each and every day. Open your eyes to the riches at your fingertips ... seek the knowledge that will remove your blindness.

Our orders were for a number of us to take one of the king's finest carriages to Bert's estate, and accompany him as he traversed the area. It was not clear to us why our services were required or why the king was loaning one of his best carriages normally used exclusively for royalty, but this was ordered by the king for as long a period of time as Mr. Smythe deemed necessary. Our duties, we were to find, would be required one or two times a week for a number of weeks. My orders were to remain in the carriage at all times ... a task I found quite unusual. I preferred the open air riding atop one of the king's many beautiful horses. Inside the carriage, I had but a small oval opening through which to view the scenery.

The ride was an easy one that took four royal guard horsemen and myself a moderate distance outside the city. The Smythe Estate stood proudly atop a prominent hill overlooking many acres of thick green grass and large oak trees. A river surrounded the sizable estate on three sides, with the side fronting the road lined with a high stone wall covered in thistle. These natural and man-made barriers, along with a number of armed men in Bert's employ, effectively barred entry to any would-be trespassers. After following the river for quite some time, we then traveled alongside what seemed an endless expanse of stone wall. One could not see what lie on the other side, nor could one safely scale the wall to peer over, for all the thorny vines covering it. The only entrance was a solitary massive iron and wooden gate guarded at the midpoint of the wall.

Once granted access through the gate, we were led by a very well-dressed gentleman along a winding roadway into the heart of the property. To each side of us were many fat cattle grazing without regard to our passage. The roadway led us past lush pastures and hay fields, through an area of dense trees, and eventually into the clear at the base of a hill. Surrounding the hill was another stone wall that was only tall enough to keep the livestock contained. Our escort opened a gate made of wooden staves allowing passage past the shorter wall. Our dirt and gravel roadway turned to cobblestone as we ascended the hill, which led to Bert's home. The roadway ended in a sweeping circle in front of the home, with a smaller drive leading around the end of the house and downhill out of sight.

The home itself was an impressive creation rising four full stories on the very highest point of the hill with the front looking immediately over a broad expanse of clipped grass, flowers and sculptured bushes. One could view the entire estate and beyond from the upper balconies. On either side of the cobblestone walk leading to the main entrance was a pair of beautifully crafted wooden stallions that appeared as if they were in full gallop. Behind the main house strategically placed on its back side were a carriage house, work buildings, and a collection of small stone cottages that were apparently occupied by those under Bert's employ. These structures were strategically placed among the trees in a way that allowed them to blend into the landscape.

There must have been a veritable army of servants required to maintain the premises. Besides the upkeep of the house proper, the grounds required considerable attention. The lawn carpeted the entire hilltop, while tall shade trees intermingled with flowering shrubs and rose bushes could be seen everywhere in-between. We found Bert standing outside on the cobblestone courtyard fronting his home. Although I had seen Mr. Smythe on many occasions from a distance, I hadn't realized how large he was in physical stature. He stood well over six feet two and was very broad across the back and shoulders. His hair, clipped close on the top and sides and allowed to grow longer in the back, was coal black and curly. This man could stand his own ground with not a soul for protection. If, in fact his personal security was a concern today he certainly had sufficient men under his employ who could do just as well. Why, then, would the most elite of the king's army be needed for his protection? Despite this apparently illogical tasking for our duties, our charge was to escort Mr. Smythe wherever he wanted to go, and for as long as he required our assistance ... this we did without comment. It was not our place to question the judgment of the king ... only to obey his orders. I could not help but find the whole affair very intriguing, although I questioned our purpose only in my mind. It seemed rather odd that we, the most elite of all the king's men, would be escorting someone for just an excursion through the countryside. Regardless, this man was one of great wealth and influence who had dealings involving great sums of money. His safety must have been the king's concern for a very good reason ... we could only ponder over what that reason might be.

Upon seeing Mr. Smythe, I remembered seeing him as one of a select few who were with the royal party during the competition, although I was assured Bert was not a member of the royal family. When he saw me among the others, he instantly recognized me and told me that it was at his insistence that I would be riding in the carriage. This would be the first of many occasions for me to accompany Bert, both inside the king's carriage, and as a guest in his home. You would expect someone of Bert's standing to be arrogant and self-serving, however I found him to be just the opposite. He was giving and genuinely interested in me and my interests. I would come to love him like the older brother I never had and to hold him in the highest regard all the remaining days of my life. For, you see, it was Bert who would become my mentor and teach me the secrets of gaining great success and wealth ... *secrets I will share only with you, my sons and daughters.*

After Mr. Smythe gave his head man some last minute instructions, He climbed into the passenger compartment of the carriage with me following behind. The carriage was fully enclosed with curtains that were drawn over the windows to block out the damp English weather. Two small oval crystal windows on each side of the rear seats allowed one to view the outside world. Otherwise, the view from the compartment was totally obscured. The interior was a masterpiece of craftsmanship, lined with soft leather and hand-polished oak; decorated by solid gold accents. Bert, at his insistence, rode in front facing rearward while I sat opposing him. The driver rode outside and above us on a perch high enough to see over everyone riding in the escort. I was uncertain what to do or say, so I simply sat quietly. Bert was first to break the silence by asking a number of questions. He asked such things as where I was born and raised, noting that he believed me to be Welch. How could he possibly know that the home of my mother and father had been in Wales? "Because you have the courage of a lion and the tenacity of a bull!" He remarked. I wasn't too certain if that was intended to be complimentary. Not once in the conversation did he talk about himself or his great achievements … he only asked questions about me. When he was not asking questions, he was commenting about me in ways that made me proud to be who I was.

Hear what I am about to say, my sons and daughters. Of all I have or will say to you, this is paramount. No matter how successful you may or may not become, it is not important in the eyes of others. To them, they are all that is important: their homes, their children, their professions. If you are to win the respect and admiration of others, do so by always speaking freely about them in a positive manner, and never speaking about one's self. Treat whoever shares your presence as if they are the most important people on earth.

This is how Bert treated me since the beginning of our friendship, and to this day, I would follow him to the very ends of the earth!

Our journey took us throughout the country. First we stopped at a place where large numbers of sheep were collected. Most of the sheep had been recently sheared, and appeared thin and naked without their heavy woolen coats. Bert had me remain in the carriage while he walked among the pens where many men sheared the remaining sheep. After awhile, he returned with two handfuls of freshly sheared wool. He had me look very closely at the fleece and asked me what I saw. I gave him the reply he expected: I saw simply two handfuls of wool. He then pointed out to me how the individual fibers possessed many waves, indicating how fine and valuable the wool. Fine wool, used for weaving expensive articles of clothing, had fibers with smaller and greater numbers of waves in a finger-length than did course. Sheep with the lower valued course wool would be set aside for slaughter, their single clipping of wool made into blankets or clothing worn by commoners.

We remained at the sheep farm until the last of the fine wool was clipped and men collected it into large bound bundles to be loaded onto ox-driven carts. Bert inspected a number of the bundles to be certain that none of them had the courser wool mixed in with the fine. When he was satisfied with the lot, he counted out a number of gold coins that he gave to one I assumed to be the owner of the sheep. The sheep, it seems, were in fact owned by Mr. Smythe, as was the land where they were raised and sheared. The man who received the gold was one who Bert had brought into his sheep trade, trained, and then entrusted the sheep to the man's care. The man was rewarded for his efforts as if the sheep belonged to him. In this way, Bert did none of the work, and shared in the rewards with the one who was doing the work. It was a simple but very effective arrangement. At shearing time, Bert would purchase the quality wool at a fair price, then allow the rejected sheep to be used to feed the herdsmen's families. This particular shepherd was one of many working with Bert on such a partnership. Bert's shepherds were taught how to raise sheep, but more importantly, they were shown how to teach others the art of sheep raising and encouraged to have partnership arrangements with even more shepherds, thus duplicating and expanding Bert's talents. In this manner, everyone who was willing to learn was allowed to prosper according to their own merits as owners ... not as common laborers.

People will always give more effort to endeavors that reward them for the quality and quantity of their work. An owner will willingly work long difficult hours without ever needing oversight, while the common laborer must constantly be prodded and can never be left unattended!

Bert simply offered his would-be shepherd's three alternatives: "Are you ready and willing to begin now?" "Are you willing, but need a few days to consider my offer?" or, "Do you wish not to be included?" Bert was selective in who was given the opportunity to make one of the three choices … not everyone took advantage of his offer, but most did. Those who did became wealthy according to their individual efforts. Bert was generous in the portion he gave back to his shepherds; they in-turn were generous to their shepherds.

As Mr. Smythe walked among the men, I noticed he talked with them in the same manner he had with me. He asked about their families, he knew the names of all the men and each member of their households … every individual he touched came to love and respect him. Through the diligent efforts of all these people who possessed and passed on Bert's genuine love and respect for others, everyone was greatly enriched, and Bert became exceptionally wealthy.

My sons and daughters, please pay close attention to these all-important truths. You might earn enough working under someone's employ to supply your basic needs, but you can earn much, much more if you will be independent and work for yourself. To become wealthy, you must go one step further by engaging others under your leadership and training; you will never achieve higher levels of success and wealth until you multiply your efforts through the labor of others. To gain the cooperation of others, you must allow them the opportunity to become enriched in proportion to their results. As simple as this appears, most men will prefer the servitude of a peasant to the uncertainty of working independently. Seek out those who share your vision and who thrive on gaining the rewards of their own independent efforts. Then finally, help them to succeed. In so doing, everyone is enriched.

Many shepherds were visited that morning, and much gold and silver passed through Bert's hands into the hands of others. It appeared to me that it was because of the considerable gold we were transporting that warranted our presence. We would learn that this was not at all the reason. People were very accustomed to seeing Bert travel throughout the land without the escort of the royal guard, and with much gold in his possession. Why an escort was needed for this particular trip and others to follow would remain a mystery for a while longer.

The remainder of our duties that day took us to other herds of sheep, other shepherds, and more bundles of newly shorn wool. Not once did we encounter anything that would raise our suspicions, although we were on our highest alert for possible danger. We were still at a loss as to why we were needed to guard Mr. Smythe, but ours was not to question the orders of the king. We would escort Bert on several more occasions, and on each of those occasions, the routine would be the same. We would bring with us one of the king's finest carriages to Bert's estate, then escort him as he went about his many errands. On every occasion, I would accompany him inside the carriage. Over the course of several days, I would gain insight into a world I had only heard about beforehand. Our friendship and discussions would continue long after my official duties had ended. On our final trip, we returned uneventfully to Bert's estate and bade him farewell.

In due time, our curiosity would be satisfied. My comrades and I had been acting as decoys while the king, was in fact, stealing away inconspicuously to a secret location. In all of the trips with Bert, we were thought to be escorting the king, so the king could conduct secret meetings unnoticed. The subject of those meetings was so sensitive that utmost care had to be taken to conceal the king's whereabouts. At every stop along Bert's many trips, I was required to remain inside the carriage. This was to give the appearance that Bert was traveling with the king ... outside of the coach, one could not discern my silhouette from that of the king's. I wouldn't realize what my role had been until later when I would also discover the purpose of all the king's secret meetings. Randall and I were in no danger while escorting Bert, however we would one day encounter unspeakable horrors ... a day far distant in our future.

While riding with Bert in our many excursions, we talked about how he became wealthy from very meager beginnings and the part God had played in his great success. Over many years, I would learn to apply these simple truths to become one of the wealthiest men of my time. These principles I now share with you.

Principle I. Give Back to God.

Ask yourself, "Why is it that some men are blessed far beyond their needs, while others scrape for their very existence?" God's treasures are vast, yet he entrusts them only to those who are good stewards. As you become more skilled in handling God's property, He will allow you greater amounts to watch on His behalf. How does one become a good steward of God's property? It is commanded by God that you give back to Him ten percent of everything you have gained. This is not an option! You <u>must</u> return back to God a ten percent tithe, and you must do it willingly, faithfully, and joyfully. If you cannot be trusted with a small portion, how can He trust you with more? Therefore, do this ... at any time you have been blessed with an increase, count out the required ten percent BEFORE you have used any of it for other purposes. <u>The portion due God must come first.</u> First before expenses; first before you give that which your king demands as his tax; and first before you feed and clothe your family. Once you have separated out the first ten percent, convey your tithe promptly into the hands of those doing God's work. Now understand this: God does not reward you for the giving of your tithe. You have already received His blessings of life, basic shelter and your daily bread ... your tithe is required to give thanks unto God for these blessings. Fail to give your tithe or delay it, and God will take these blessings (however modest) from you. And because you have not proven yourself to be a good steward of His property, God will reduce His future giving to you.

Just as God will reduce His blessing when you fail to give His commanded ten percent, He will bless you with an increase in His future giving to you when you give more than He requires. God accepts this extra as a special gift … if it is given without the expectation of anything in return. What you give as a gift, you will receive back up to a hundred fold! However, if God chooses to return nothing back to you, remember that you intended it to be a gift and expected nothing in return! But God is a generous and loving God. He will always give you more than you deserve, whether it be gold, property, time, or love. This is why you must always give thanks unto God for all He has given to you … He can never be repaid, nor does He expect to. All He really expects from you is a portion of your money, property, time, and your unconditional love. He gives each of us a portion of His infinite goodness in unequal shares. Of all the wealth in the Universe, His most treasured possession was His only son, and He even gave Him to us as well!

Principle II. Give to Others.

I cannot explain why it is, but those who cling tightly to their gold and silver will have it pried forcibly from their grip. There will always be unexpected expenses that will drain the life from one's treasure chest. Yet those who use their resources of time and possessions to help others cannot give it away fast enough … it will come back in multiples. There are those who expect all of their daily sustenance be given to them, even though they are fully capable of work. Let these leeches starve! It is the unfortunate ones who are more than willing to fend for themselves but cannot, that deserve your generosity. These will be truly and eternally grateful, whereas the derelicts will condemn you for not giving them more.

And when you give to others, do so without drawing attention to the deed. Do so in secret, and God will bless you many times over (if not in this life, in the next); do so publicly and you may get brief public recognition, but nothing more … you have received your reward. It is far better for your good deeds to remain a mystery … if you can, in fact, keep them a secret! Once you become unselfish in your deeds, you will become caring in all your dealings with others. You will be respected and loved by all.

Principle III. Give to Yourself.

A wise shepherd will always keep a portion of his lambs to increase his flock. The rest he will sell or slaughter to feed himself and his family. If he were to sell or slaughter all of his lambs each year, there would be an abundance of food, wool and gold the first year and possibly the second, but eventually his flock would diminish until not a single lamb would remain. In the end, he and his family would be without the food or clothing his flock once provided. Conversely, the more lambs he saves back, the more he and his family will have later on. The wise shepherd knows that to save back a portion now would require some sacrificing of comfort for awhile ... a sacrifice rewarded many times over for the rest of his and his family's lives. As you reap your harvests, always save back enough for seed to replenish and multiply your storehouse!

So listen carefully, my sons and daughters. As you receive the fruits of your labors, give first to God his required tithe of ten percent. Secondly, give a portion as a gift to God for His work. Thirdly, give a portion to those truly in need. Then fourthly, save a portion to invest towards the future ... it is your decision how much to save, but remember that little saved will produce little, whereas much saved will produce much. After you have followed these instructions, then, use the remainder to pay your expenses. No matter how much you reserve for your expenses, you will always have expenses that consume all that is available! Control your expenses by limiting how much you have available to pay them. Live within the boundaries of this final remainder and you have conquered the concept of thrift!

Principle IV. Be Not Indebted to Others.

One must recognize that there exists two varieties of debt. There is one that adds to one's personal possessions, and another that multiplies one's storehouse. Each is treacherous in their own way. The first kind is the passion of fools. You must realize that there is no limit to man's wants. In his impatience, the foolish man borrows to acquire now, things he does not need instead of waiting to purchase at a later date without borrowing.

At first, the fool is overjoyed with his new purchase; he displays it proudly so all can see. But eventually the excitement dims and he longs to possess something else. Each time, it becomes easier to borrow, but harder to repay. As the days, weeks, and months go by, the fool will give up most of his weekly earnings to pay his debts, leaving little for food, clothing and shelter for him and his family. He becomes entrapped with possessions he no longer wants but cannot sell for even a portion of what is owed. He is forced to work longer and harder to avoid starvation, falling ill from the burden. So sad it is that he will became too sickly to work and will no longer be able to repay his debts. In the end, all of the fool's possessions are taken to repay only a portion of his debts and he loses all he had, to soon die a pauper.

What might have been wiser? First of all, had the fool waited until he had saved the required price, he would have had time to re-evaluate the wisdom of the purchase. A wise man would not have considered any purchase wise that is too great in magnitude in relation to his earnings. To purchase something "wanted" rather than "needed" is not necessarily wrong … if one first obeys the principles of giving and saving, has sufficient remaining for necessities, and has earned the right to the prize. To become indebted to another man enslaves the debtor and enriches the holder of the debt. It is a choice that makes one man rich while making another man poor. Of the two, who is better off?

The other form of debt multiplies one's storehouse. One must be very shrewd in the ways of business to understand how to profit from borrowed gold. The wise sheep owner will add to his flock by borrowing gold to buy more ewes. But the extra wool will, over time, return more to the shepherd than what was borrowed plus the usury fees. The danger comes when one becomes greedy, borrowing far too much in an attempt to fill the storehouses faster. The debt holder will always require something of value to secure your debt. If the debt is too great, you will risk losing all when unforeseen events occur. Instead, only borrow what you can afford to repay under the worst of circumstances. It is far better to gradually increase your wealth and keep it all, than to become wealthy only for a short time and lose it all to the debt holder.

Principle V. Use Your Money Wisely

Another fool saves every spare farthing over a number of years, hiding it away for none to see. To accumulate this treasure, the man spends nothing and gives nothing. His clothes are tattered and long in need of replacement; his home is a shelter intended for swine; his food ... the spoilage of the marketplace. He lives a miserable life and does so alone. In the end, he will accumulate much gold, but will die of starvation. This man, like the debtor, is also a fool because he sacrifices to the extreme to amass a fortune, but could have much much more if he uses the money wisely; his could be a life far more befitting of one of affluence. At the very least, he could live far better than he does or he could make life better for others around him.

So what does the wise man do? He treats the road to wealth as a well-planned journey. In the beginning, he carefully measures the money he has after giving and saving. From that amount, he buys what he needs for a modest, but reasonable living. He avoids debt and postpones his wants of the present so he can live very well in the future. To do this, one must know the difference between a "need" and a "want". These are needs:

> *water for thirst*
> *food for sustenance to satisfy hunger*
> *clothing to the extent needed to cover ones nakedness and give warmth,*
> *shelter to protect from the elements and intruders, and*
> *fuel for warmth and for cooking*

Anything more is a "want". But wants are without limit. All things desired but not needed are "wants". These are a few:

> *wine for drink*
> *eating to excess or of foods for indulgence*
> *dress for appearances sake*

shelter that is greater in size or grander in design than is needed,
and the fuel needed to heat it

As his savings accumulate, the wise man holds back a portion for the unexpected events that everyone must face. He then uses the extra of his savings to buy assets that will multiply his wealth. In the early years, the investments within his grasp may be very small. However, many small transactions made over time will allow successively larger transactions. All the while, he remains free of debt.

Where the fool becomes a debtor to have now, the wise man uses his resourcefulness to increase his income so that what he wants (above what he needs) is paid for without sacrifice. Is it wrong to want? Only if "having" what one "wants" takes away from God or others according to these principles. It is never wrong to be rewarded for diligent and honest effort. Those who are wise use the power of their wants to intensify their creative energy; making the objects of their wants the rewards for achieving ever increasing financial goals. Just as importantly, the reward must be constrained so that it is in proportion to the achievement … the prize must never consume one's seed or too much of the gain. After reaching a goal and earning the prize, the wise man's investments continue to produce for him! He then moves on to a higher, loftier prize. The ultimate prize is total freedom from both debt and labor owed to another.

Principle VI. Do Not Be Afraid to Dream

The most successful are those who see what "can be", vividly in their minds then take action to make these images real. At a very early age, a certain young man would lay under the trees in the deep green grass that grows thick and soft in the shady meadows, and watch the clouds move across the sky. Those who knew him considered him lazy and treated him with contempt. He ignored the jeers and laughter, all the while seeing images in his mind of great and wonderful things.

One day, he became fascinated by the swaying of the trees in the wind, and he imagined the tufts of clouds above him being propelled by the force of the treetops. As his imagination worked, he envisioned a contraption that, instead of clouds, propelled stones at great distances. With the help of his brothers, he fashioned from young straight trees and leather bindings the device he saw in his mind's eye. His vision became the catapult used to win wars against our enemies. Like the young man, many have the ability to dream ... to see in their minds what can be ... but dreams are only passing thoughts without action. Take time from the drudgery of your daily chores to dream, then work to make things happen.

All great things once began as a thought ... an idea ... a dream in someone's mind. The grander the dream, the greater the accomplishment! Never limit the size of your dreams and never cease to achieve what you imagine! The difference between the rich man and the pauper is measured only by the size of their dreams and their effort ... nothing more! Dream the impossible and do what no one else dreamed possible.

Principle VII. Use Your Time Wisely

In the beginning God created the heaven and the earth. And the earth was without form, and void and darkness was upon the face of the deep. And the spirit of God moved upon the face of the waters. And God said, "Let there be light": and there was light. And God saw the light, that it was good: and God divided the light from the darkness. And God called the light Day, and the evening He called Night. And the evening and the morning were the first day. (Genesis 1: 1-5)

After God created the day, He used each of the next five of them to create the sea, the land, the trees, the grass, the flowers, all living creatures, and man. On the seventh day, He rested. This is how God intended for us to spend our time; planning our days and working creatively to make the world a better place, but taking time from our work to rest and reflect on what we have accomplished. Always follow this principle and you will always live a blessed life.

Principle VIII. Be of Good Character

A knight is admired and respected by all who know of the goodness in his heart. But all despise the man who is deceitful and dishonest. Had Bert once in his long years of dealing with others, cheated a single partner, the deed would have been told and retold throughout the land. All who were his partners (and all who might be) would be distrustful and reluctant to enter into any new agreements. In time, Bert's shares would decrease and eventually cease all together. It is one of life's certainties. Do a good deed to someone and it will be retold to five others ... do a bad deed to someone and it will be retold to twenty! Spoken another way, it is far easier and quicker to lose a good reputation than to gain it. In all your dealings always do what is right ... do not even leave the perception that you are cheating another. Once one has been tainted with the title of a cheat, one will never be known by any other name. Always live a life of integrity, even if it means foregoing a little extra in the short term. But how does one know what is right? This is the simplest of all answers to give ... always follow God's teachings, and seek His guidance in all matters.

Principle IX. Learn

Look around you and you will find thousands of hard working souls, yet why do those who work so hard have so little? Could it be that hard work is only one part of the equation? A question ... who among all craftsmen earn the least for their skills? Is it not the common laborer? Then who among all craftsmen earn the most? Is it not those whose crafts require the greatest skill and knowledge? There are in fact three types of professions that earn more than the average: those that are so disgusting that it repels most people; those that are so dangerous that only the most steady of nerves would assume the risk; and those that are far too complicated for those of average knowledge and abilities. Many professions have elements of all three. But the most important element that decides wealth is knowledge! Should you strive to have the most distasteful, dangerous, or complicated of all professions? No! But it is vitally important that whatever profession you find to be the most rewarding, you become an expert and excel in that field. You become an expert by continually learning more on your chosen subject, then you excel by applying your newfound knowledge to your craft. Is it not true that those who are the best in any given profession are also the most in demand? You become the best by learning and doing!

So how do you learn? There are but three ways: You may choose to learn by trial and error. This is the slowest and most difficult way to learn. You may never in your lifetime uncover all of the skills for your chosen profession through repeated attempts.

If you can find someone who is the best at your chosen craft, make every attempt to follow their example and observe their unique methods. If this is not possible, seek writings from those who have succeeded and learn from their insight. If the best in your craft is willing to teach you their secrets, enthusiastically accept their counsel and strive to absorb all they can share with you.

Once you have achieved the title of expert, never cease to learn and perfect your skills. There is always greater knowledge to gain.

Principle X. Be Strong

Strength comes in two forms: power and endurance. These traits apply not only to your physical abilities, but your mental abilities as well. You cannot separate the two! How does one become strong? You become strong by always striving to exceed your known capabilities. Your mind and your muscles have one very interesting thing in common, the more you work them, the stronger they become. Conversely, the less you work them, the weaker they become! Strength comes from daily efforts to excel, allowing time each day for rest except on the Sabbath, then as commanded, do no work on this day. Randall was my mentor in achieving great strength. Here lie the simple secrets to his enormous size and physical capabilities:

At a very early age, Randall suffered a near fatal fall that made him a cripple. He walked with great difficulty and had a twisted disfigurement of his head and shoulders. As he grew older, his condition was the subject of much ridicule by others. But Randall chose not to be a cripple. He found that certain efforts, such as hanging from tree limbs and pulling upward with all his might, (although painful) would loosen the tightness that bound his head and shoulders. He found that the more he moved his legs the easier it became to move them faster. At first he walked only a short distance. In time, he was running several miles. He persisted in working his muscles with longer distances and heavier weight until one day, no one dared ridicule him. If Randall, who was once a cripple can become physically strong, how much stronger can you become? His was a journey that demanded hard work, but had he not possessed the mental toughness to push through the pain and extend his capabilities, he could not have endured.

By becoming strong, you can overcome adversity. This is essential to your success, because success will not come easily … if it did, most would be successful. To become strong, follow Randall's example. Continually strive to become physically stronger by working both your mind and your body past the barriers that exist only in your imagination!

Principle XI. Practice Good Habits

Grandfather taught me the skills of combat. Those skills were but a few basic movements repeated many many times until the execution of those movements came without conscious thought. All habits, whether good ones or bad, started out as conscious action that was repeated over time. The secret to success in any endeavor is to choose good habits that will move you closer to your dreams, then practice those good habits repeatedly until they become a part of you.

What are good habits that will make you wealthy? Practicing these principles until they become a part of your very being! There are many more good habits that are worthy of acquiring. These habits will become apparent to you as you change and grow. Never cease the habit of changing and growing!

Principle XII. Plan Your Battles in Advance

A knight never goes into battle without a plan of action. This is also true for achieving one's goals and dreams. Bert disclosed to me one of his greatest secrets of success … the secret of planning. The results are very powerful, yet the system is so very simple. Bert kept a written list of his dreams and his daily efforts to achieve his dreams. His dreams were the most worthy of achievements possible that brought great excitement to him whenever they were brought to mind. A date was firmly set for achieving each of his dreams along with a step-by-step plan to get there (the difference between a dream and a wish is a dream has a date and a plan for making the dream a reality). His plan contained all of the sequential steps that were necessary from the start of the journey to its conclusion. Then at the beginning of each day, Bert would review his plans to decide the efforts needed for that day. At the end of each day, he would again review his plans and assess his progress. As each goal or dream was achieved, Bert would add to his list with even greater dreams and goals. The process is never ending … always plan your future, otherwise, you are simply reacting to the situations you face, rather than progressing to an envisioned destination.

Principle XIII. Open Your Eyes to Opportunity

Opportunity in abundance surrounds us every single day, so why do we not take advantage of these plentiful opportunities? The answer lies in our inability to recognize opportunities as such. Bert was a master at uncovering the greatest of opportunities. How did he do this? He did it by first having a Dream and a Plan! When you have a burning desire to achieve great things, and you have planned the steps necessary for achievement, then your eyes will be opened to opportunities that bring you closer to your ultimate destination.

Later on in life, I dreamed of possessing a grand estate like Bert's. I began by writing down all of the features I desired in this beautiful place. It would have a river around it with a tall hill in the center where I would build a grand home. The home would be made of rock and oak with many stories and rooms. I possessed a special journal where I recorded these items either in words or in sketches. As I journeyed throughout the kingdom, I passed many tracts of land, but I only "saw" the ones that were by the rivers and held a tall hill in its center. After many years of searching, planning, and dreaming, I located the perfect match near Dorchester. It was not available for purchase at the time, but was sold to me for a very fair price upon extending an offer to the owner. Had I not held the dream and envisioned in my mind the parcel of my dreams; had I not been looking for the envisioned parcel, the right one would not have appeared; had I not known which property was the right one, the offer would not have been made; and without making the offer, the opportunity would not have presented itself. The secret? Dream, plan, prepare, be watchful, then ACT!

Principle XIV. Teach Others

There are two ways to multiply your abilities and thus, your wealth. One is to work longer and harder, the other is to teach others your skills and employ them to multiply your accomplishments. By relying on your own labors, you are limited by the time available and your physical endurance. By teaching others, you are limited only by the number of people you can employ and train. It was a hard lesson for me to learn that to succeed as a knight I had to become a leader, respected and followed by others. I gained that respect not by demanding results, but rather by teaching them the skills that allowed me to succeed. Likewise, Bert grew in wealth by leading others to become successful. He did so by teaching those who were worthy, the skills and principles for becoming wealthy. By sharing your gifts with others, you will be enriched, and when your life has concluded, your gifts will live on forever! Of all the things you must share with others, teach the gift of teaching! Then your talents not only grow in amazing leaps, they become eternal!

Changing Priorities

King Richard, I'm told, was a genius in the making of war, but lacking as a statesman. He had many enemies who were striving constantly to undermine his political authority. There were some, like Bert, who were absolutely loyal to him, but there were others who only pretended to be. Thus, King Richard staged a hoax. The many excursions we made to meet Bert and escort him around the kingdom was to lead people to believe the king was, in fact, along on these visits. While we went from place to place, the king was secretly watching the treachery of those in his court who meant to do him harm. The day would come for the king to deal harshly with his enemies. There would be much shedding of blood ... some of it ... much of it, by my hand.

As I took up arms against the king's enemies, the fighting waxed heavily on my soul after a number of years. I longed for a life like Bert's where I could be free to live without the burden of obligation and constant danger, even if it meant giving up my dream to become a knight. I wanted a family of my own. When my mind was free to think of things other than matters of the sword, I would picture Dora and how she had come to my rescue and nursed me back to health. I don't know exactly when the feeling crept over me, but I acquired a painful longing to be with her when she reappeared in my life in a chance encounter. It would be my turn to come to her rescue!

This rescue was of a much tamer variety, with no ones life held in the balance. By sheer happenstance on one of the many times escorting Bert, our carriage and entourage passed Dora as she walked innocently along the roadway. She was returning home after visiting a cousin. With Bert's permission, I had the driver stop the king's carriage just ahead of her. Dora, was brought by one of my guards to the carriage and told the king wished to speak with her inside. She nearly fainted when she looked up after bowing and saw me smiling back at her! Bert graciously allowed her to accompany us for the short ride back to her home ... I can't quite describe the feelings that came over me in seeing Dora again. Something about her was different; she wasn't the spindly youth I had left behind nearly two years earlier ... she was now a beautiful young woman. This chance meeting would lead to many more that were intentional. Deep inside, I always knew Dora was intended to be my wife, but marriage was not possible so long as I was in the king's service.

After many months of agonizing over what to do, my final decision was to forego my dreams of knighthood, leave the king's service and marry Dora. *My sons and daughters, the world is full of those who could be your wives and husbands. Trust God to lead you to the one He has chosen for you. Wait! Do not be impatient! Your success and happiness is not only fostered by the right mate, your success and happiness is possible ONLY with the right one! Learn from the teachings of Solomon and choose a companion of character and purity of heart. You will know when the one appears that is chosen for you. Once you've found her or him, reach your arms around them and never let go. When I found the one I knew in my heart to be the one chosen for me, I learned that she was not mine, nor I her's. We were chosen for each other.*

The choice to seek my fortune outside of the royal guard was very uncertain, as I had nothing in the way of possessions on which to build a life for Dora and eventually our children.

My sons and daughters believe in what I'm about to say. In all things, whenever you give something up, something of equal or greater value will replace it. This is true about your possessions, your position in life, or even your dreams.

In giving up my life as a swordsman, I gained a wonderful life with Dora and wealth beyond my greatest expectations. I have God to thank for bringing Dora back into my life, and Bert for adding me to his group of teachers. By applying the principles Bert had passed on to me, I would expand my reach beyond the few sheep put under my care. There were only a few shepherds under my direct contact, but with the efforts of those few, Dora and I would eventually surpass the wealth that even Bert had accumulated in his lifetime.

The dream of becoming a knight was replaced by the vision of a loving family with whom I could share the grandest of estates. The new dream, shared by Dora, became a vivid reality. The estate was like Bert's in many ways ... a river alongside over three thousand acres with a grand home resting atop the tallest hill (the children were uniquely ours!). We found the property in the heart of Wales near Dorchester with the River Thames running alongside. The home was a majestic stone marvel built by a former nobleman who lost the favor of the king and met an untimely death. Even though I was still in my younger years, my wealth and my relationship with the king made it possible to acquire the property well within my means.

In all my dealings, I followed Bert's teachings. As Dora and my wealth grew, we always gave to others in need, becoming known to those around me as the "Benevolent Lord of Dorchester". With all of the many tasks of running the estate handled by others, I was totally free to use every hour of the day to my choosing. It would have been so easy to grow fat and lazy ... there was literally nothing of a physical nature required of me. But instead, I continued to train in my skills, growing in strength and stature. This still gave me ample time to share with Dora and our many children. It was a grand life but one that could not last. God ... and King Richard still had other plans for me.

PART IV

Courage, Victory and Honor

The Quest for the One True Cross

I believe Dora understood why I had to go on this quest, but you, my sons and daughters, were young children and could not. It was a very sad and gloomy day when the King's messenger appeared at my gate. The messenger was none other than my close friend and companion, Randall. The King was enlisting the aid of all his loyal war-fighters to regain safe passage of Christian pilgrims to Jerusalem through the lost lands of Palestine and to reacquire the "One True Cross" artifact; both lost to invading Muslim armies after the second Crusade. The King was preparing a third Crusade to retake all that had been lost. My grandfather had faced a decision very much like mine and chose to again serve in the king's army. Upon his return, he found much of his possessions lost and his wife afflicted of blindness. My father made the same choice and never returned. I now realized that neither Grandfather nor my father had a choice. Once called, a warrior must serve ... it's an unbreakable oath of duty.

Unlike Grandfather, I parted with a reassurance that my family would be well taken care of. I was not so certain of my personal fate on this long and dangerous quest to a strange an unfamiliar land. Armed with my father's sword and my shield, I left my beloved Dora and each of you, my sons and daughters, sobbing at our gate. Randall and I would have much to talk about, but we would ride in silence for many hours after our departure.

My sons and daughters, please believe me when I tell you that of all the wealth you may possess, nothing in this world is more valuable than the

*love of your family. Cherish every moment for you do not know the hour of
your departure nor your return … if ever.*

Although I was quite strong, my skills of war required some attention. With Randall's help, I trained day and night to regain lost speed
and agility. By the time we departed England's shores, I was ready to
fight and if need be, die for this quest. Such is the oath of the soldier.

After suffering seasickness throughout the journey, our arrival to the
Lands of Palestine was on one hand a welcome relief, but on the other,
one of grave concern. I knew little of our Muslim foes except that they
were a dangerous people who possessed the lands once walked by
Christ. At first we met with little resistance, but as our quest pushed
southward towards Jerusalem, we were met by swarms of Turkish
fighters. They at times, exceeded us in numbers but lacked our disci-
pline and skills in combat. In my final battle, I became separated from
the other Crusaders and stood alone surrounded by several of the
enemy. I closed my eyes as if I had given myself to them. When I
sensed their attack, I evaded the thrusts of their swords, then with my
eyes still closed and while they were coiling for a second attempt, I
swung my sword with all the might I had inside of me and decapitated
three with a single stroke. I could not kill all five at once, and the
fourth and fifth, struck before I could return with my own blade. My
quickness of movement averted fatal blows and I remained on my feet
to fend off another volley of thrusts, but I was severely wounded and
losing a considerable amount of blood … nearly passing out from the
rapid turning movements. The last I remember before all became dark
was the heads of my attackers falling to the ground at Randall's feet.

◆   ◆   ◆

The battle had been won, but we did not achieve ultimate victory.
King Richard and his army would venture no further south, instead
choosing to return to our homeland. He had been abandoned by his

allies (or rather, he had offended them and lost their support), making it impossible to proceed. My injuries are horribly painful yet still I am alive. At times I drift in and out of awakening, seeing only the sky above and the sea beyond. While awake, I embark on this final quest to write these entries in my journal. Whenever I am enveloped by darkness, my sons and daughters, I see only your faces and your mother's before me. In fear that my life may end before I complete my journey homeward, I struggle feverishly to scribe these final thoughts and feelings. God, I pray Thee ... give me strength to finish this final quest. Give me the strength to complete this, my Will and Testaments, and if it be Your will, allow me to carry my writings to my sons and daughters myself. Your will be done!

PART V
Finality and Immortality

Last Will

It has been many days and nights since our departure from the Holy Lands. My wounds are deep and I am unable to stand. Every movement sends spears of lightning hot pain through my back and sides, yet I continue to write this final will and testament with a clear mind. Now all I feel is pain; those from my injuries minor compared to the one in my heart. I deeply miss my family ... Dora, children, I love you so very much. To Dora, my faithful, I give you all my worldly riches ... may your days be long and free of want. To my sons and daughters I give you the knowledge in these testaments. From my words, I shall live on through you.

My sons and daughters please hear these words and take them to heart. I now reflect upon a lifetime filled with adventure, victories, wealth, honor, happiness, and intense sadness ... the happiest of times experienced with the one and only woman I've ever loved and each of you ... the saddest of times; here and now. Through these final testaments of my life, I share with you, my sons and daughters, the secrets that will give you all these things and more ... including intense sadness if you so choose. Of all I have achieved and acquired, the one thing I cannot pass on to you is one more additional day of life. Today is all I have remaining ... your days are also numbered. But I thank God for giving me the strength to see this day through and to complete this final adventure. We do not know when our time on earth will end, so use very wisely the little time you have allotted. No matter how long your years on this earth, they pass ever so quickly. Do not waste even a moment of it; yet never hold onto it selfishly. Like wealth, life is meant to be shared. There remains one last secret that I must share with you. With my last breaths, I give to you, my sons and daughters, the one single truth that bears the most valuable of all the knowledge I can convey to you:

You will consume a lifetime in search of adventure, victories, wealth, honor and happiness. In the end, (and only then) will you understand (as now have I), that happiness does not come from <u>reaching</u> your dreams. Happiness comes from reaching <u>for</u> your dreams. It is not the destination that makes life rewarding, it is the journey!

After you have achieved the boundless wealth and success I know you will possess, this final over-riding principle is the secret of achieving happiness and meaning in your lives. Try to understand the words I have written, because my thoughts are fleeting and my hand weak. So, my sons and daughters, follow the direction only God can show you; never limit the size of your dreams; achieve success beyond your dreams; and above all else, live each and every day enjoying your journey through life.

My final wishes are simple. Learn from my mistakes so you need not repeat them. Learn from my successes so you may go far beyond my grandest achievements. As you gain wealth, share it with others. Even more so, teach others how to succeed, however, guard these secrets from the hands of those who would rob you of your success. Let no one other than those of a pure heart see or possess the contents of this journal. Do not believe that this will change the world. There will always be those like my good friend Daniel, who will know more than anyone else and will not follow these instructions. There will be those like George who will aggressively seek wealth then hold onto it for self-serving purposes. The Bruces of the world will be content with what they have and will not wish to endure the pain that accompanies success. Then there will be the Randalls of the world who will live to serve others. People who will listen to your instruction, will succeed only by their own labors. If only the Randalls of this world listen to you, learn from you, and follow you, you will be greatly enriched, and this world will be a greater place for all mankind.

Signed
Sir John Holcombe

Retrospect

◆

Conclusion by J. Arthur Holcombe

This story is based upon the life and times of my true ancestor, Sir John Holcombe (the first) who was of Welch ancestry and served in the third Crusades under King Richard the Lion-heart, of England. The Welch people, living in the mountainous regions of the British Isles, were a sturdy breed known for their tenacity and independence. Sir John, whose existence is recorded in the "Visitations of England", served in the War of the Crusades to Palestine, where in the Third Crusade (1187—1191 AD), he beheaded three Turkish Muslims with one stroke of his sword. For this act, he was finally granted his lifelong dream by being knighted by King Richard.

The Third Crusade was an attempt by Christians to regain Jerusalem and safe passage of Christian pilgrims through the Holy Lands after it had fallen to the Muslims in the latter part of the 12th Century. King Richard and his men (who included Sir John), traveled to Palestine by way of Messina, Sicily (to meet with an ally, King William of Sicily), then on to their first battle at the Island of Cyprus. After conquering Cyprus, King Richard and his Crusaders arrived at Acre (located between modern day Tyre Lebanon, and Haifa Israel), on June 8, 1191. King Richard never reached his planned destination of Jerusalem, failing to achieve his ultimate objectives of reconquering the Holy Lands for Christianity and regaining possession of the relic, the One True Cross. On October 9, 1192, King Richard was shipwrecked while returning home from battle and was imprisoned by one of his many enemies, King Leopold of Austria. History tells us Sir John Holcombe died of wounds he received in battle, however it is not clear if he actually died in the Holy Lands or some time later. Sir John now rests in the oldest abbey in England, Abbey Church of Dorchester. The Holcombe Coat of Arms, depicted on his crypt and at the beginning of this book, bears the inscription "Veritas et Fortitudo", which means "Truth and Courage"; an appropriate motto for one who lived his entire life in search of truth and courage, and ultimately found both.

The events I've depicted are a combination of actual historical events, myth, and in some cases, fabrication, but is deeply rooted in fact. The principles of knighthood and success have been passed down through the ages and stand as truth, as was Sir John's existence as a Knight and Crusader. My hope is that you will prosper from Sir John's principles on your path of *Truth and Courage*.

The End

An Addendum

✦

Inspiration for the Path of Truth and Courage

J. Arthur Holcombe

Now that you've read "The Path of Truth and Courage", I hope your life has and will be greatly blessed by the knowledge I've shared in this book. Since the original publication in 2001, many readers have written back to tell me how much their lives have been enriched from reading "The Path of Truth and Courage". They have also asked where the inspiration came from for the story. The story itself is a fictional account of the life of Sir John Holcombe; the guiding principles are real and many of the events in the book were inspired by my own personal real life experiences. Most of the inspiration for the story actually came from some of the strongest and wisest people I've ever known who have influenced my life profoundly in one way or another.

Now allow me to share with you in this passage, another story about some of those special people.

In the late 1940's, my mother, Dorthy, (the youngest of three girls and one boy) and my grandparents, moved from Oklahoma, to a small farm in the Ozarks of Northwest Arkansas. They shared a four-room frame home that had a fireplace for heat, a wood cook stove, and a pull-chain operated light bulb hanging from the ceilings of each room—all four of them. Water was drawn from a hand pump in a shed outside, and a "privy" was at the end of a long trail away from the house. Instead of a refrigerator, they had a cellar where canned fruits and vegetables were stored. I believe my mother was only 15 years old when she married my father; I was born about a year later. I was told by my paternal grandmother, that my father had been in the Navy in World War II. He didn't have a college degree, but had almost enough credit hours to receive one. When he married my mother, he was a businessman in a nearby town. I only have two childhood memories of my father (when I was around the age of three): one of a family outing to a gentle stream known as Osage Creek; a happy occasion where we parked the car by the stream, took off our shoes and waded in the cold clear water. The other was at another family outing by another stream, only my father wasn't among the family members enjoying the warm summer day. I don't remember much about the occasion, except that my father came later but parked his car way off in the distance and just stood next to it. I recall running over to greet him—then as soon as I got there, he gave me a quick hug and said goodbye. He left me standing in the grassy field with tears streaming down my face—it was the last time I would see him as a child.

In the book, Sir John's father died valiantly in battle, but in my real life story, my father left us to start another family. Memories are muddled as I'm sure too many changes in a young life can cause a great deal of confusion. However, most of what I recall of my early childhood were events that came later after we had moved into my grandparents' home. After my father left; my mother would find out shortly afterwards that she was pregnant with my sister, Susie. There weren't a lot of choices for a single mother with only a 10th grade education and two small children. So, my sister and I were placed in our grandparents care while my mother tried to earn a modest living at anything she could find. As in the story of Sir John, my grandparents farm was off the beaten path and very austere. They sold their farm in the 1960's when my grandfather's health worsened, and moved into a tiny frame house on my Aunt and Uncle's farm. The new house was actually smaller than the old one, but unlike the old house that still had no running water or other modern amenities, the new one did. Grandfather lived only a few months after their move; my grandmother lived there until she passed away nearly 30 years later.

My grandmother was one of the most amazing women I've ever known. She lost her sight in an accident when she was a young mother; yet was able to move as freely as anyone who wasn't blind. Financially, my grandfather barely survived the Great Depression in Oklahoma. He was a mechanic-turned-farmer and at one time he and my grandmother owned a service station-grocery store. In the years I spent with him, he was dying from emphysema after years of smoking and working in the Oklahoma cotton mills. My grandmother would become my confidant and secret advisor who would share her experiences, her wisdom, and her feelings with me over my formative years.

Fast forward 12 years. My mother had remarried and had a household of five children to care for. I was a restless, bored 15-year-old with no direction in life and with a great deal of uncertainty as to my role in that household. I desperately needed a change, so when I couldn't stand my circumstances any longer, I asked—no demanded—to move out. My mother and stepfather reluctantly agreed, and from that moment on, my life would never be the same.

When I tell people I left home when I was 15, I was being honest, but to be totally honest, I have to admit that I really wasn't totally on my own. With no place to go, my Aunt Sylvia and Uncle Frank took me in, on their 90 acre farm in Northwest Arkansas.

Along with my grandmother, we all started a new life when I joined them. My new family was to outsiders, a collection of people with handicaps. Uncle Frank was both physically and mentally disabled. He walked with the aid of a cane and was showing initial stages of dementia. My Aunt Sylvia was the rock-solid foundation of my new family. Her wit was sharp as a knife and her will was unshakable. She, too, was lame as a result of a farm accident. She had a broken ankle that never healed correctly, but you would never hear her complain. Sylvia only considered her lameness as an inconvenience; it might have slowed her down a bit, but it couldn't keep her down. Until I appeared at her doorstep, she was the only one who could physically do anything to keep the farm running. Farm work is hard and dirty for a man, but this woman had been doing all of the heavy chores along with the usual domestic duties of the household. With their farm and small dairy herd being their only means of livelihood, they could barely afford to take care of their own needs, let alone mine as well. So, to make it possible for me to stay with them, I had to produce more than I consumed—and I consumed a lot!

It's true what they say, "home isn't a place, it's a state of mind",—it's actually memories of a special place in a special time. I lived with Frank and Sylvia every day for the next three years of high school and called the farm home until I graduated from college five years after that. To this day, I will always remember the farm as my home. I thank God every single day for those eight short years because as I lived with my aunt, uncle and grandmother, I really learned how to live.

My aunt's name was Sylvia Vivian—her middle name literally means "to live". Life was hard for her—very hard. However, her motto was "it's a great life if you don't weaken." Every morning, I would hear her singing as she put together a breakfast fit for a king. You could hear her happily singing her way through every day—rain or shine. I never knew a more positive or determined woman in my life. She found something good in everything, everybody and every situation. For example, whenever I was discouraged, she would tell me to listen at the sound of a bird that nested in the fields nearby. "Do you hear what he's saying?" she'd ask, "He's telling you to 'Cheer-up! Cheer-up! Cheer-up!'"

I moved to the farm in July, the hottest month of the year. I was small, weak and—well—a bit lazy. Sylvia had a garden large enough to feed a family of three, so with my arrival and an extra mouth to feed, there was a challenge. But challenges didn't seem to bother Sylvia. She just repeated another of her favorite sayings: "when there's a will, there's a way." Or to repeat her favorite Bible verse: "All things are possible through Christ which strengthens me (Phil 4:13)." She found the way by putting me to work. After a good night's sleep and a great breakfast, she would work my butt off all day long! She solved the food shortage by having me plant an acre of potatoes. All summer long, it was my job to weed and care for those potatoes. At harvest time, I got to hand-dig that entire acre of potatoes. It was hard, hot sweaty work, but the potatoes fed us all winter long. We also had a variety of fresh vegetables from the garden, milk from the dairy cows, eggs from the chickens and fresh blackberries that grew wild in the thickets. For meat we would have a steer butchered or we would dress a few of the chickens. Finally, she found work for me on neighboring farms to bring in money for my clothes and for my school supplies in the fall. The work wasn't any easier off our farm as it was on. The work she found was hauling hay, shoveling out chicken houses or pushing a lawn mower over acres of farmhouse yards. By the end of that first year, I was no longer small, weak or lazy—but I was very tired and sore most of the time.

When I appeared in Sylvia's life, I don't believe things could have been any worse for her. Since almost all of our sustenance came from the farm, our expenses were low, but there were still needs that had to be purchased. Essentials like feed for the milk cows, propane for the home, gasoline for the tractor, seed, fertilizer, and so forth. The bills were getting paid, but there wasn't much left over. We found out later my uncle had a serious drinking problem that he had been hiding for years. He had been siphoning off what little money extra there might have been to pay for his habit. Unfortunately, I was the one that caught him—and even then, he hid it so well I didn't discover it for a couple of years. What I found first was a shortage of cash in the family account when I was learning how to do farm bookkeeping. I also noticed my uncle's violent mood swings—something I learned later in life that was very common among those with a drinking problem. Then there were the remarks I overheard from my friends at school about my uncle's frequent trips to visit one of the locals. One day, I caught him returning from the local who turned out to be his supplier. I also found his "stash".

I was working in the hay loft where I could observe without being seen. I can remember being angry beyond description watching him tip the bottle upward and guzzle down the amber liquid. I don't have a problem in the least with those who drink occasionally. I'm not a tea-totaler myself. What Sylvia and I had a serious problem with was that we were struggling to stay alive and scraping for every single penny. Alcohol was a luxury we couldn't afford—especially since it was Sylvia and I earning those pennies. More than that, we really had a problem dealing with was the ugliness that came out of my uncle after the alcohol wore off. Physically he wasn't much of a threat, but he could be very temperamental. After I shared what I knew with Sylvia, she realized why things had been the way they were. She also knew what she had to do to solve the problem. This was one of the few times I saw her cry. Her's were tears of both anger and disappointment. Sylvia and I together confronted Frank with his half-empty bottle later that day and got him to admit he had been taking money from the milk checks to feed his habit. Although he admitted it, he tried to defend his drinking as his only remaining pleasure. There was never another word said about the subject. If he ever had any more drinking binges, we never found out about it. The cure was pretty simple; Sylvia took away the vehicle keys and the checkbook. She also had a talk with his supplier. I have no idea what she said to Frank's friend who had been selling him his liquor, but I do know Frank never saw him again—nor did my uncle ever leave Sylvia's sight for an instant afterwards.

By many standards, we were living in abject poverty. But we never went hungry and we never accepted handouts—and somehow, we never realized that we were underprivileged. Sylvia taught me how to see the world through her eyes; and how beautiful that world was. Because of her encouragement, I was active in high school activities and learned how to achieve. In 1968 I graduated from high school just at the right time for the Viet Nam war and the draft. I accepted my pending alternatives and prepared to enlist in the Air Force before I was drafted into the Army. Sylvia wanted me to go to college. My grades were good enough, but I had no money for college. That didn't seem to matter to Sylvia because, "when there's a will, there's a way." Of the few times I tried (always in vain) to avoid what she wanted me to do (which usually involved chores she wanted me to do), I had never seen her as resolute as she was on me going to college. Since my arguments were all about money (or the lack of it), her shot across the bow was a simple request, "if you get a scholarship, then will you promise me you'll go to college?"

My logic was sound at the time, but Sylvia lived totally on faith, so logic didn't go far with her. The easiest way to get her off my case was to agree to go to college if I got a scholarship. I believed at that time in my life, that I had a better chance of solving world hunger than I did of getting a scholarship. Darned if the 4-H Club of Arkansas didn't come up with a $250 scholarship. $250 won't buy much today—and guess what, it didn't back then either. But that didn't matter to my Aunt Sylvia. Once you made a promise, you kept it—especially if you made that promise to her!

There were many people who inspired different parts of this story. But the majority of the secrets to success in "The Path of Truth and Courage" were inspired by my Aunt Sylvia. Thanks to her, I have succeeded beyond my imagination. I did go on to college—and finish (and did so on my own resources), then went on to get a post-graduate degree later. After graduating college, I was commissioned into the US Air Force, and would serve as an active duty officer, then as a reserve officer, with thirty years total time to my credit. I would retire from the Air Force Reserves as a Lieutenant Colonel. Today my business interests are many and life keeps getting better and better. If I were to have any regrets, it would be that I didn't spend more time with Sylvia in her later years. There was so much more that I could have learned from her that could have saved me a lot of hardship along the way. In her final weeks in the hospital, she was unable to speak and, because she was heavily sedated, rarely aware of her surroundings. After she passed away (she was in her 80's), I longed often to hear again her words of encouragement—words I would hear many times while she was alive in our weekly phone conversations. She left me a little golden chest that I keep as a reminder of her and what her life has meant to me. In that chest is her old tattered bible with earmarked pages and underlined passages. After her funeral, I opened the front cover to find a passage noted there in pencil. The passage was Philippians 4:13. She apparently felt that passage was so important that it should be prominently identified in the very front of her Bible. Through that little note, Sylvia had, in fact spoken to me again and had left with me all I needed to go on, without her to encourage me. Look up the passage and you'll understand how. If I can find the words to someday tell Sylvia's story in a way that will touch others as her life has touched me, then you will understand why.

If you would like to find out more about the author or order additional copies of this book or other works of J. Arthur Holcombe, please visit our website at:

www.truthandcourage.com

978-0-595-21088-6
0-595-21088-0